STOP POSTING!
START MARKETING!

STOP POSTING!
START MARKETING!

How successful businesses market themselves on social media, while others just post

Joe M. Sanders

Table of Contents

Introduction

I was born in December of 1980, a few days after John Lennon was shot. People born around this time are hard to define: we're not quite Generation X, not quite Generation Y, and not quite *fill in the blank*. Technology-wise, it was a pretty intriguing upbringing. Early on, I remember using floppy discs, playing vinyl records, and writing papers on a non-Windows® computer. My family even watched movies on a VCR we rented from Sears. Eventually, we progressed to high-speed Internet, DVDs, laptops and iPods®. By my freshman year of college, I was one of the cool kids using a cell phone, and there weren't many of us. So, as a professional marketer (and just as a human being, for that matter) I have had the benefit of growing up during a time of staggering technological evolution.

In the early 2000's, I ran a concert promotions business with some friends, and we thought it would be a good idea to use social media to promote shows. Back then, social media had a different name and it was called Myspace®. Because Myspace didn't have an advertising platform for small businesses, we had to do our best to promote the shows manually. We paid a team of high school kids to spend up to six hours a day finding, friending and messaging users who liked a specific band in order to advertise a concert. It took forever, but it worked.

A few years later, I landed my first real marketing job as a marketing manager for one of the largest and highest-volume independent restaurants in the United States. Around this time, Twitter and Facebook had just begun their descent into marketing for small to mid-size businesses, and I wanted in. I remember walking into a meeting with about ten restaurant managers and the two owners. I did some research and prepared what I thought was a pretty good a marketing plan using these flashy new digital platforms. I presented my case and waited for a response. One by one, they all said, "No." (LOL). They obviously had no idea what I was talking about, and who could blame them? Social media marketing was in its infancy stage. Back then, I'm honestly not even sure that I fully understood what I was talking about. As time went on, the rest of the world was jumping on board to this new world of promoting your business on social media. Thankfully, my company jumped on the bandwagon too, and so my journey into professional digital marketing had officially begun.

Fast forward 15 years and thousands of posts later, I decided to start a digital marketing agency. Since then, I've worked with literally hundreds of businesses in various industries ranging from insurance, to trades, to architects, to wedding venues, to bakeries, to financial planning, to *you name it*. I want to be clear that digital marketing as it stands today truly is the Wild West. Within the industry, there are almost no regulations and very minimal standards of practice, meaning there are innumerable ways to execute digital marketing campaigns. This means there are a vast number of ways to succeed, and an equal number of ways to fail.

I wrote this book to help business owners and marketers to think more critically about digital marketing. I believe that all marketing problems, including digital ones, can be solved through a properly developed strategy, but we must first take a step back and think critically about every aspect of the marketing equation. I have been referred to as a "digital marketing expert" or "digital marketing guru," but I shy away from those titles. The reason? How could I, or anyone, consider themselves an expert on something that changes every day? Trust me when I tell you that Mark Zuckerberg is not texting me, asking for my permission when he makes changes to Facebook. Yes, I may know a lot about digital marketing, having studied it for so long. Yes, I may have spent countless hours executing digital marketing strategies every day for years. However, this is the aspect of digital marketing that you must accept: it is going to change, and it is going to change often. What doesn't change, fortunately, is the discipline of marketing itself.

Prospective clients often ask me "What is your area of expertise"?

I always say "Marketing"

"But what digital platforms are you *really* good at?" they ask.

"Marketing platforms," is my typical reply.

"But what social media platforms *work* the best?" they continue.

My response: "The ones that you market on the best."

As we dive into this book, I want you to start thinking about the fact that it doesn't matter which digital platform you choose for marketing; it's the execution of the marketing strategy on that platform which makes the marketing successful. This is a relatively new concept for some, especially among those who choose to market by creating accounts on several platforms with no goal and no strategy. My argument is that if you create a proper marketing strategy and go through the appropriate marketing equations, you can literally market anything to anybody pretty much anywhere. This is not to say that every marketing effort is successful, but when you understand *why* certain strategies don't work, you can start to think like a marketing person: a skill of tremendous value. Remember, the goal is not simply to be able to master one platform or another; it's the ability to market well on *anything*.

In this book, I will lay out the best ways to create digital marketing campaigns for your business. As I do, consider how my recommendations will work for your specific situation. There's a handy-dandy worksheet in the back of this book with questions pertaining to each particular chapter. I want to encourage you to follow along with me by thinking about and answering these questions as we go.

Similar books on digital marketing, many of which are excellent, focus heavily on topics such as where to click or where find an application. Don't get me wrong, these can be great resources, and having a certain level of comfort with your chosen digital marketing platform has enormous benefits. However, digital marketing platforms change all the time, and many of these resources become obsolete pretty quickly. A vast number of free, online resources will walk you through each platform and show you how to use any number of functions or applications. By using these and other resources to "keep up with the game," so to speak, you should be able to figure out the "how" of what you're doing with minimal effort. Therefore, I won't waste your time, or mine, by delving into those topics. Besides, I remember sitting down with a client one time, very excited to show him how awesome I was and how much I knew about the advertising interface of a particular social media platform, only to find that the site I wanted to show him had changed that very morning. It took me by surprise. This sort of thing happens from time to time, and you'll just have to adjust to the new layouts and configurations.

I intend to provide you with something even more valuable than instructions on where to click to do this or that; I intend to provide you with the *why*. By learning these skills, you'll be able to develop a digital marketing strategy and execute successful campaigns regardless of the platform. Cast your focus on marketing strategy and sound marketing equations, and forget the idea that certain platforms work while others don't. Let other people focus on their particular business, and you focus on what works for yours. Take the time to do it right, and you'll be surprised at how powerful this thing we call marketing can be.

Please refer to the glossary in the back of this book for definitions of marketing terms. There is a worksheet in the back of this book that I highly recommend using.

1

You Don't Have Social Media Problems, You Have Marketing Problems

This is not a book about how to successfully run Facebook Ad campaigns that will make you a million dollars overnight. In fact, this book is not going to be very technical at all. The truth is, the technical skills required to run successful social media marketing campaigns are not as hard to learn as you may think. Don't forget that social media and digital marketing providers want to make money too, and they strive to provide user-friendly interfaces that almost anyone can learn and use. Therefore, a person with even a hint of marketing know-how should be able to acquire all the technical skills they need in order to advertise on social media interfaces by watching a few hours of YouTube videos. Sure, there are a few aspects of Facebook Ads Manager® that might make you nauseous (and me too!), but don't be fooled into thinking that your technical skills, or lack thereof, have anything to do with your ability to be a successful marketer. Some of the best marketers in the world know very little about the depths of social media functionality. What they *do* understand is how these platforms work in relation to their brand, their business, their budgets, and their bottom line.

Marketing hasn't changed, and it never will. This is because people haven't changed. So, until we do, we are stuck with our selfish, reluctant, non-trusting, and easily distracted selves. The goal of marketing has always been to get someone to pay attention to a business, purchase a product, or interact with a brand. In any case, the goal is to influence people and build relationships. Business owners and even marketers tend to forget that every email address, Facebook profile, and user account they have access to is, in actuality, a real person. I've worked with some professionals over the years who own and run marketing companies but who actually know very little about marketing or how to influence and build relationships with people. They can, however, create a fantastic app or website, or set you up with a very sophisticated digital advertising campaign, both of which are very valuable skills. Unfortunately, many of these types of technical geniuses fall short in putting together a complete marketing strategy in order to solve the marketing problem. They are, quite frankly, (and pardon the cliché) a "one-trick-pony."

Marketing is a living, breathing organism that encompasses all aspects of your business, brand, and even the people in your organization. Nowadays, most companies focus heavily on digital platforms to achieve marketing success, and they should. Yet marketing your business on Facebook, Instagram, Twitter, or Snapchat is no different from buying TV spots to sell cigarettes on the "I Love Lucy" show in the '50s, putting up billboards around town to promote your new ice cream store, running a direct mail campaign to sell garage doors, or sponsoring the Little League baseball team in your community. The basis of these actions is marketing, plain and simple, and focusing on anything less is where most of you are getting it wrong.

Like many things in business, successful marketing is not easy, as the discipline requires knowledge and mastery. Many people think of marketing as a lottery ticket when they should be thinking of it as a 401(k). While some companies do gain overnight fame and fortune in the marketing arena, the majority of successful businesses play for long-term growth, something that requires adjustments and corrections to market conditions along the way. Remember, marketing is not a science; it's an art. So, when Facebook digital campaigns don't produce the results we want, when we put up promotional signs in our business and people ignore them, and when we spend thousands of dollars on an automated Google Ads campaign that doesn't work, we then question the relevance of our entire business, our business model, and ourselves.

Marketing is the process in which most business owners want to spend the least amount of time, energy, and resources, but it is, in actuality, the very thing they think about the most. Specifically, when dealing with social media or digital marketing, this lack of comfort can become a complete aversion. The response, and supposed solution, then, of many business owners is often to use a flashy advertising pitch about Facebook Ads or an automated/out-sourced software program that seems to do all the work for you. For some reason, many people can't seem to grasp why this ongoing ritual of throwing money toward new platforms and new marketing managers over and over again doesn't seem to work. What they're missing here is not a lack of marketing, but a lack of understanding of how marketing works.

I have worked with hundreds of business owners over the years, and I can't tell you how many times I've heard:

- "We posted our event on Facebook, but nobody showed up."

- "I never click on ads, so nobody else does either."

- "That's not a good enough return on my investment."

- "The report says I reached a lot of people with my ad, but it didn't produce any results."

- "There is simply no way to prove that digital marketing works."

These and other popular sentiments about social media marketing stem from a syndrome I'm going to call **The Magic Function Approach.** This approach assumes that a business or product that has not been previously positioned on a particular marketing platform should produce positive results simply by virtue of appearing via the said medium for the first time This is not true at all. Without a sound marketing strategy, simply posting something on your social media pages means absolutely nothing and, typically, it will produce absolutely nothing. This approach to marketing is nothing new and has plagued business owners and marketing managers for decades.

Over the years, many business owners have complained to me that their marketing doesn't work for one reason or another, and yet they have absolutely no way of *quantifying* whether or not that marketing strategy worked in the first place! I recall one conversation with a CEO who called me the day after his company had launched gift card banner ads on various digital marketing platforms. He called to say that his company had not sold any more gift cards on the first day of the campaign than the day before and that he felt he had wasted his money. I responded by asking him if he had ever seen an ad for a Lexus on TV. He said yes. I asked him why he didn't stop what he was doing the moment he saw one of those commercials, drive straight to the nearest Lexus dealership, and buy a new car.

This kind of emotional reaction by the CEO is a common one. It comes from a place deep down inside when a person means well and is trying really hard to solve a complicated problem with a process they do not fully understand. Although the situation with the banner ads does not have a simple solution, I intend to use this book to help you gain perspective on this and similar situations. If you stick with me until the end, you'll be able to troubleshoot and think through this and many other marketing-related problems. For when we approach marketing from a strategic position, we possess the ability to evaluate, quantify, and adjust in real time. Hopefully, you will be able to use this knowledge and apply it to running sound marketing campaigns, regardless of the platform.

Before we move on, there is one more idea that we must clear up and bring into the light. Please don't take this personally, but *nobody cares about your business*. Nobody cares about your event. Nobody cares about your promotions and, trust me on this one, nobody cares about your social media posts. Nobody cares but YOU, maybe the people you work with and possibly your marketing company. Never before in history have we been bombarded with so many messages in 24 hours; it's simply staggering. A significant reason why people fail to attract attention or gain traction on social media is that they underestimate how much people just don't care. When you finally grasp this idea, it's the perfect place to start.

Every business, product, and event needs a champion: someone who can make it happen. Hopefully, that champion is you. However, be cautious about getting wrapped up so deeply in your business world that you lose the ability to relate to your audience: the people who probably know nothing, or at least very little, about what it is that you want them to do. They usually have no cognitive foundation relative to your idea: something *you* have in abundance. In fact, some of you are so obsessed with your product or business that you're sweating it out of your pores. This is a dangerous situation that usually leads to overly complicated contests, overly restricted coupons, and far-reaching, convoluted reward programs. You must change your perspective from someone who will do whatever it takes to make a buck, to someone who is a customer advocate: someone who wants nothing more than for customers to not only interact with and purchase the product, but to do so in a way that builds a positive relationship and may eventually convert the customer into a brand ambassador.

When marketing something (anything, anywhere), always remember that you have to relate and communicate your ideas in the fastest, shortest, most uncomplicated way possible, or people will not pay attention. Pretend you're explaining your concept to a kindergartener. Think about it: if you had to give directions to your house to a kindergartener, how would you do it? Would you use a lot of complicated details and words, or would you use a more visual and straightforward approach? That is what your customers are: they are kindergarteners concerning your business, your ideas, and your promotions.

It is also important to note that digital marketing campaigns and social media are only one part of a whole marketing strategy. For example, if a company needs to sell more widgets to a target audience, then *that* is the marketing problem. The best solution for solving that problem may be to use digital marketing, including social media, but that is only one function of an entire marketing strategy. The tools and information required to solve a marketing problem are classic, have been around for years, and will be taught and used throughout this book. I intend to help you understand how to apply traditional marketing strategy to modern marketing problems. So remember: you don't have social media problems, you have marketing problems. It just so happens that the platforms on which you want and need to market are digital and are ever-changing. Because of this, an excellent strategy would be to build a solid foundation upon which you can market your business using any digital media platform. Because nobody really knows what the next big social media platform will be, but good marketers really don't care.

2

How To Succeed At Marketing (Even When You Fail)

Think back to 6th-grade science class and try to remember when you first heard about the scientific method. If you were like me, it probably went in one ear and out the other. However, the process is actually the basis of a sound marketing strategy. The scientific method is as follows:

1. Ask a Question

2. Conduct Research

3. Construct a Hypothesis

4. Test Your Hypothesis

5. Analyze the Results

The point in conducting an experiment using the scientific method is to *learn* about the problem as opposed to actually solving it. Of course the goal is to solve the problem, but by design, the scientific method *assumes* that you don't know the solution. Instead, this process allows us to *use* a strategic trial and error approach to *eventually* solve the problem. Why is this important? Because problems typically do not have one clear-cut solution, and they usually require time and effort to solve. The scientific method assumes that you are most likely going to fail, but the data you collect in the process will help you to solve the problem eventually. I realize that many of you already know what the scientific method is, but how many of you are actually using this method (or something similar) when it comes to your marketing? Perhaps you are simply trying to solve the problem every time and failing, all the while ignoring the most valuable steps in the process.

As in all aspects of life and business, some degree of failure is an inevitability, but as I always tell my team, "If you're not failing, you're probably not trying very hard." You have to get out there and try, with failure being an assumed and acceptable part of the process. When our mindset is such that we are not afraid to fail, we can think more creatively and with more freedom. Don't get me wrong, failure is not the goal; being successful in our endeavors *is*. However, when we attack our marketing problems from a strategic, organized position we gain knowledge from our failures, which has tremendous value. The problem lies in approaching a problem without a strategy. In that case, we learn nothing; we simply fail and have nothing to show for it.

The scientific method is the basis for sound marketing strategy and can be broken down in a modified form to fit any marketing equation. Some of you may have heard of the "4 P's of marketing," which is another standard tool. The 4 P's are typically referred to as:

1. Product - What is your product?

2. Place - Where customers can buy your product?

3. Promotion - How your customers find out about your product?

4. Price – What is the cost of the product to the customer?

The 4 P's help us to organize our business into four major categories, all of which are necessary parts of our marketing efforts. The idea is to focus on each category independently, defining the SWOT's (Strengths, Weaknesses, Opportunities, and Threats) of each. Thinking of your business in this way is helpful and can be expanded to the "7 P's," which include People, Packaging, and Positioning. While I do find the P's useful, they fail to capture the rational process by which we fail, learn, and eventually succeed. Therefore, I am going to introduce a new 5 Step system which will form the basis of marketing strategy in this book. This system resulted from running social, digital, and traditional media marketing campaigns. It was designed for business owners, not necessarily just marketing professionals. The steps are listed below, and I will discuss each in detail as the book progresses.

1. **Find the Right Audience**

2. **Create the Right Content**

3. **Promote Your Business as a Brand**

4. **Use Ample Resources**

5. **Analyze the Results**

While some of you may think that this process is far too simple to be effective, I would say that you're probably making the process overly complicated and likely have been for years. I am always amazed by the way some of the most brilliant and successful business people I know will spend hours and hours going over every penny related to labor, cost of goods sold, and utilities etc. However, these same professionals will blindly spend thousands of dollars on almost any person or product related to marketing which, on the surface, seems to make sense to them at the time. Then, when this strategy doesn't produce the desired results, they spend very little time analyzing *why* it didn't work. In the end, they just decide that the person or platform they were working with is, and will always be, a bad idea. However, they can't prove this, because they never had a system in place by which to evaluate the original plan in the first place. It's a catch-22. Consider the following scenarios, for example.

BUSINESS: PIZZA RESTAURANT

Marketing Problem: Increase lunch business Monday-Thursday

Hypothesis: Facebook Ads can be used to increase weekday lunch sales

Scenario #1

Bill, the owner of the restaurant, decides to buy Facebook Ads to grow his weekday lunch business. He concludes that $10.00 per day should suffice. He hangs up an 8.5 x 11" flier in his dining room promoting lunch specials that he got from his graphic designer. Bill takes a picture of the flier, posts it on his Facebook page, and clicks the "boost" button for $10.00 per day for the next four days: Monday through Thursday. At the end of the week, Bill pulls the data and notices that his lunch sales are just the same as the week before. Bill decides that Facebook Ads do not work to grow sales and never uses them again.

Scenario #2

Bill, the owner of the restaurant, decides to buy Facebook Ads to grow his weekday lunch business. Bill talks with his management team, bartenders, and servers to get a clear profile of the typical weekday lunchtime customer. Bill also drives around the area and notices a few office buildings within about a 5-minute drive of his restaurant. After speaking with staff, Bill decides on the following target audience for this campaign:

- Men and Women

- Age: 25 - 55

- -People who work within 5 miles of the restaurant

Bill reaches out to his graphic designer and asks her to create some Facebook Ads showing busy people at work who could really use a slice of pizza and a drink to get them through the day. He suggests using something funny that might catch their attention. He requests that she highlights the major intersection where his business resides and suggests that they have a "15 minutes or it's free" guarantee on all lunch orders. He asks her to include pictures showing off the restaurant's delicious pizza and cozy interior. Bill asks one of his tech-savvy servers to pull data from Facebook, and they find that there are about 50,000 people who fit his target audience profile and that it is going to cost about $10.00 CPM (cost per 1000 impressions). Therefore, Bill decides to spend enough money to reach 25% of the audience (12,500 people) for six weeks. At $10.00 per CPM, this amounts to about $125.00 per week spent on Facebook Ads. He chooses to run his ads from 8 am – 2 pm, Monday through Thursday only.

After week #1, Bill's lunch sales are flat. Week #2 is just the same, but he reached 12,000 people in his target audience this week. During week #3, Bill notices a small group of people from one of the targeted businesses dining at his restaurant for lunch. As Bill engages with the customers, they mention having wanted to try the restaurant for some time. They tell him that they decided to dine there today for no particular reason. Raving about the pizza, they ask why Bill doesn't deliver to their business, as most days they can't leave the office at lunchtime. He informs them that he is happy to deliver and gives the employees a stack of menus to take back to the office. Bill contacts his graphic designer again and asks her to change the ads to say, "Fast delivery and 10% off this month if you work at XYZ Corporation." Week #4 sales are flat again, but he is now reaching 15,000 people a week for the same amount of money as the weeks before because some of the employees he met have been sharing and commenting on his posts. By week #5, XYZ Corporation calls and places an order for ten large pizzas and salads and asks if Bill can make this a once-a-week thing. He agrees.

Obviously, scenario #2 is the ideal situation. While Bill may not have wholly solved his weekday lunch lull, he did learn a great deal about his audience, which helped him to begin to solve his overall marketing problem. By running an organized and strategic marketing campaign, Bill was able to quantify and adjust in real-time, bringing him closer to his goal. I would also argue that the most crucial aspect of the entire campaign was the fact that Bill learned not only who his target audience was, but also what sort of content to create for them. Had he continued to spend money marketing his cozy dining room to businesspeople working near his restaurant, he would most likely have never increase his lunch sales. Only by adjusting the content of his marketing campaign (which in this case evolved from cozy dining room to quick delivery), was Bill able to create the right content for the right audience. Unfortunately, Scenario #1 describes the most common way that people fail at marketing. Below is an analysis of each using the 5 Step process I introduced earlier.

Scenario #1

Step #1 - Find the Right Audience

Bill spent very little time trying to decipher his ideal target lunch audience. When Bill "boosts" his Facebook Ads, he does so blindly, without considering any demographic or geographic information. Bill assumes a "set it and forget it" mentality and does not attempt to relate to any real person in his target audience.

Step #2 - Create the Right Content

Bill uses whatever creative material he has on hand for his promotion. Fliers that hang on the wall are designed for hanging on the wall, not for Facebook Ads. In many cases, advertisements like this will not stand a chance of being boosted on Facebook, and the ad platform will reject them. Bill also does not consider what time of day his ads will run.

Step 3 - Promote Your Business as a Brand

Taking a picture of a sign on the wall and posting it on a social media platform will typically produce a low-quality image which does not represent your business well and will most likely be difficult to read. Bill does not include any high-quality pictures of his food or his dining room in his promotions. This makes it difficult for him to positively influence anybody who has never been to the restaurant before.

Step 4 - Use Ample Resources

Bill assumes that $10.00 per day is the right amount of money to spend for no particular reason other than the fact that it sounds reasonable to him.

Step 5 - Analyze the Results

Bill analyzes the sales data, which is accurate, but does not take the time to analyze results from the marketing campaign itself.

Scenario #2

Step #1 - Find the Right Audience

Although Bill doesn't spend money on research, he uses his resources effectively to define a target audience for his campaign. Bill also determines precisely how many people in his target audience are actually on the platform he decided to use (Facebook), in order to increase his lunch business. Bill understands that the Facebook audience consists of real people and that relationships matter. Therefore, he makes every effort to interact with them.

Step #2 - Create the Right Content

Bill has his graphic designer create content specifically for his Facebook Ads campaign. Throughout the process, he adjusts the creative content to relay what he believes to be the best message and creates visuals that he believes his target audience will relate to. Bill also considers the time that his ads will run in relation to their content. He concludes that ads promoting pizza at lunch to this selected audience will work the best from about 10 am – 2 pm during the week.

Step #3 - Promote Your Business as a Brand

Bill includes pictures of his food and dining room with a funny message. These images speak volumes about his brand: he is a local pizza restaurant with a neighborhood vibe, casual dining room, and friendly service.

Step #4 - Use Ample Resources

Bill runs some quick math equations to figure out how much money to spend in order to ensure that his content reaches a healthy amount of the people in his target audience with his messages.

Step #5 - Analyze the Results

While Bill's sales do not increase during the first four weeks of the campaign, he notes that his ads are reaching the right amount of people, with the right message, and at the right time. Encouraged by this information,

Bill decides to stick with the campaign and adjust the messaging as needed. As a result, he sees an increase in lunch business throughout the campaign.

The approach used in Scenario #2 outlines the basis of a sound marketing strategy. Please note that I will provide an in-depth explanation of each aspect of the 5 Steps in the later chapters of this book, including exercises related to figuring out CPM's and creating enlightened marketing budgets for your campaigns. At that time, I will also break down what I believe to be the three most important words in marketing, tying all of this together. If you feel overwhelmed at this point, or if this content is way over your head, then please be encouraged because you're in the right place!

3

Two Big Ideas To Ponder

Before we go any further, I feel it is essential to have you consider two major ideas related to social media and marketing in general. I bring up these thought exercises based on my experience of working with business owners and marketers. I feel that they are helpful to consider before we start diving deeper into more practical knowledge. The two ideas are:

1. **Marketing Problems vs. Business Problems**

2. **Posts vs. Ads**

MARKETING PROBLEMS VS. BUSINESS PROBLEMS

Let's start with a story. John opened an escape room business four years ago in a suburban downtown and has struggled with driving revenue over the past 18 months: a far cry from his first two years in business where he was making great money and a healthy profit. John has three different escape rooms in his building and an ample website. John hires Julie's Marketing Company to help drive more customers to his business. Julie begins marketing the business and finds that the majority of John's competition is marketing heavily on Google and Facebook. John is not. Julie decides to run marketing campaigns on Google and Facebook and launches a well-thought-out campaign. As a result, John's escape room business improves a little bit, but not nearly as much as it needs to and definitely not enough to justify the cost of Julie's marketing efforts. Julie tries again and again and again, but she can't seem to move the ball for John's business.

Julie is a good marketer though (she's read this book, like, ten times!), and has many successful clients who adore her and refer her to other business owners. Over six months, Julie tries out and runs sound marketing campaigns, but she comes up short every time. Eventually, John puts the escape room business up for sale, and Julie hangs her head in shame. Why did this happen? I already told you that Julie is a good marketer and knows what she's doing. Her campaigns reached the right target audience with the right content that effectively represented the business's brand. She used enough resources to penetrate the audience correctly, and her analytics were reliably based on sound marketing metrics. So why didn't this work?

The Backstory: When John opened his escape room business four years ago, he was one of only six escape rooms in the entire state and the only escape room in his geographic area for nearly thirty miles. Over the past two to three years, however, over forty escape rooms opened up in the state, including two in John's town, each less than five miles away. Each of John's escape rooms (his products) have been the same for the past four years, with no updates, and John does not have any additional revenue streams for his business. During a conversation with Julie, John becomes frustrated and tells her, "Hey, I've had 30,000 people come through this place in the past four years, and people love my escape rooms. Why can't you get this to work?" Julie *wanted* to say, "Think about it, John: you *had* 30,000 customers, that's true, but those 30,000 customers have already come through. They can't give you any more money." The majority of John's customers have either attempted or completed all three of his escape rooms, and therefore they have no real reason ever to revisit the business. More so, the amount of people interested in Escape Room's is limited, and the increased competition has made it very difficult to drive revenue. Therefore, John's business problems (due to the changing landscape of the escape room industry) could legitimately be blamed for this case of marketing failure.

This isn't to say that Julie's team could not have done a better job in their marketing efforts, or that her team did not make any mistakes along the way. What it does mean, however, is that John's industry and his products (escape rooms) had become completely oversaturated. It was so oversaturated that John needed to find a way to differentiate his business and products from the competition in order to stay competitive which is something that John didn't do. So, while Julie's team made a few suggestions that might have helped to make John's business stand out, he did not listen. Julie, of course, was not privy to John's financials, his cash flow, or costs such as rent or utilities, nor is Julie an expert (like John) on the costs involved in building a new escape room or updating an old one. So, while Julie can make suggestions, she is still at the mercy of what John and his business ultimately decide to do. After all, it's John's money, not Julie's.

John refused to listen to any of Julie's or anyone else's suggestions about changing or making improvements to his business. He was convinced that all of his problems were caused by poor marketing tactics. In this case, it could be argued that poor marketing is to blame (it can always be justified). The main problem, however, was that Julie was paid to use her sound marketing skills to market a business/product that nobody wanted to buy. And the best marketing in the world can't convince people to buy something they don't want. This is a classic situation of marketing problems vs. business problems.

Cases like this arise from time to time: when you are faced with the task of marketing something that nobody wants. You must always inform the business owner of this fact, or at least your opinion, and help them to do whatever they can to fix their business problems. However, it is not

necessarily the job of the marketing manager to correct the business problems, especially if the business owners will not listen. So, when you are
running marketing campaigns that don't seem to work no matter what
you do, then yes, maybe your marketing strategy is just plain wrong, but
consider, too, that sometimes you might just be running into legitimate
business problems.

POSTS VS. ADS

In the world of social media, there is not a vast difference between posts
and ads. You need to remember that any form of social media content you
post is a marketing piece and is, therefore, also an advertising piece. Ok,
now I know what you're thinking: *so what's the difference between marketing
and advertising?* The answer is, again, not much. Think about advertising
as a function of marketing. I have a new sandwich on my menu. I need to
market it to my customers, so I find ways to **advertise** it. The advertising
is the action of showing a product to an audience; the marketing is the
idea and strategy. When it comes to posts or ads, the main thing you need
to consider is the purpose of what you're posting (the why) as well as the
availability of resources.

Every post on your social media pages needs to have a purpose. Don't
freak out; I'm not saying that every campaign is going to take an hour of
developing strategy and another hour of creating content. What I mean
is that every post you put out there needs to be a function of your entire
marketing strategy. You'll want to push some of these posts more than
others; we'll consider these ones ads. **Ads** are social media content geared
towards a specific audience that you spend money on. **Posts** are social media content that you *don't* spend money on and that achieve their value
organically. **Organic** reach refers to the number of people who see your
content without you having to pay for it directly. It's a "free" advertising
idea. Remember, though, that getting an ample number of organic users

to pay attention to your posts on social media by building a true following might take you weeks, months, or even years. So, while you might be getting "free" organic reach now, consider how much effort and investment it may have taken you to get to that point. Just like building a network of customers anywhere else, you'll need to spend time finding the right people, figuring out a way to get them to pay attention to you, and encouraging them to care about your business or products. It's not going to happen overnight, and it requires advertising, communication and relationship building.

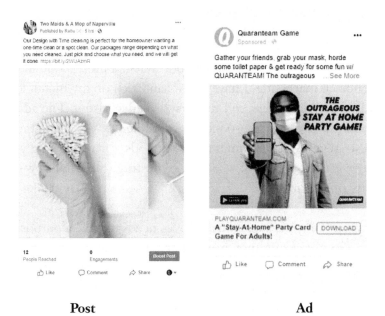

| **Post** | **Ad** |

Both will show up on a user's social media page, but the ad shows up as a result of paying money to show it to a specific group of users. Notice how the ad says "sponsored" at the top and the post does not.

This organic reach and engagement is the cornerstone of a robust social media marketing campaign. While this typically requires spending money, the investment is almost always worth it. Why? Because you are building sound relationships with real people and, just like in the non-digital world, this takes time, energy, and intention. Remember, people are people whether they're on digital platforms or not, and neither people nor marketing have really changed much.

Ask any successful business owner about their best source of marketing, and they'll no doubt tell you referrals or word of mouth... and they'd be right. Referrals and word-of-mouth marketing work best because they are based on relationships, not advertisements or marketing placements. While a prospective referral may do some research on a business before hiring them or buying their product, most referral business is easy to attain because someone already has a relationship with someone else. The basis of this is trust. So, if I trust you and you refer me to a business, then I do business with them based on the confidence of the relationship I have with you, and usually not much more is needed. This type of marketing has been around since virtually the beginning of time, or at least since human beings have been interacting with one another.

Networking always remains a prevalent practice among businesspeople because, while it can take time, networking is essentially about building relationships, and social media is essentially no different. So, when it comes to your social media content, remember that while spending money and advertising are usually essential to growing a solid following, relationships are a vital element that should not be understated. Social media is supposed to be social. Don't get too bogged down, thinking you can't be successful if you don't have a lot of money to spend. Lots of very successful companies use the element of *community management* to run amazing digital marketing campaigns.

POSTS VS ADS CONTINUED - MARKETING WITHOUT SPENDING MONEY

Community management is an approach to digital marketing whereby you spend time building relationships with individual users and groups. Some of you might be doing this already, as building relationships with people is a natural human condition. For others, you'll need to take time and be intentional with your content, just as you would attend a networking event to meet new people in the physical world. The digital version is no different. In its most basic form, you start by setting up a personal profile. You set up an account with your name and job title, post about your life, and connect with people you know. You can take this further by reaching out to people you don't know, such as a friend of a friend. Your business can also have a profile, but usually these two kinds of accounts are separate. You don't necessarily need to share aspects about your personal life, but do your best to connect like the real person that you are. While some users may be intrigued with what your business has to say, many will also be enticed by the kind of person you are as an individual. Just like in real life, though, if you want your relationship to grow, you have to spend time and energy making it happen.

As I've stated several times already, marketing hasn't changed, so if you want to get a referral from a digital source, you're going to have to build relationships with the person or the people who represent and control that digital source. It is a connection based on trust, just like any other relationship. The beauty of building trust in the digital space is that it is effortless to share information. So, if you have an old friend, or make a new one in the social media world, and someone wants to share information about your business, all they have to do is click a little button and instantly they can share your website, online store, or social media page with their entire digital network. They can also endorse this with a personal message, leveraging the trust they have with individuals in their already-established network. This is why many companies do very well growing their business by focusing on managing their relationships with real people in the digital world.

Besides one-on-one relationships, another significant aspect of community management is integrating yourself or your business into a group. **Groups,** in whatever form, are gatherings of users centered on a singular, common idea or interest. Most social media platforms have groups in one form or another, and they typically do not cost money to participate in or join. Groups can be about literally anything from classic cars, to gluten-free eating, to ice cream shops in Baltimore, or LGTBQ gardening. They are a great way to find people who might also be interested in what you have to say (or sell). Remember, though, that these groups are gatherings of real people, much like the networking group at your local BNI Chapter. So, no, they are not going to be interested in you just talking about yourself or your business all of the time or spamming them with offers and discounts. Take the time to do networking (and marketing, for that matter) the right way, by being genuine and by adding value to the group or relationship. Don't just look to add to your bottom line all the time.

So, who should you be online: yourself or your business? That's for you to decide. Remember, it's the same decision you have to make when you walk into a party full of people you don't know, meet your co-workers on the first day of a new job, or go to a networking event where you know absolutely nobody. Typically, the best way to navigate a relatively stressful situation like this is to just be you and to take an interest in other people. Don't only talk about yourself. However you do it, remember that there is a vast digital world out there full of potential clients and friends. Still, these are all real people, so the only way to build the relationship is to be genuine and intentional about building the relationship. This form of non-paid, organic digital marketing can be incredibly powerful, and when paired with paid ads and a digital marketing strategy, it can produce truly compelling results.

POSTS VS ADS CONTINUED - THE HISTORY OF CUSTOMER RELATIONSHIP MARKETING

Businesses can also build relationships with their customers and have been doing so for decades. Typically, building a relationship as a business will require a platform or tool that the company will use to manage the users' information as well as the communication. There has been a dynamic shift in the way that businesses use digital marketing to help navigate those relationships over the years, and it is ever-evolving. To help you understand this further, I am going to explain a summary of how the Facebook algorithm works, with a little history of relationship marketing mixed in. I'm choosing Facebook because it has been around the longest, has the most history, and the comments and rules regarding how the Facebook algorithm works will apply (in theory) to just about any social media site.

Customer relationship marketing is the function by which businesses provide an op-in service for their customers to receive information about the company. This type of marketing has been around for decades and started pre-internet with companies asking customers to provide a mailing address. When the business wanted to contact them with a message, they could simply mail something to the customer. The early computer age of the '70s and '80s allowed businesses to enter all of these addresses into a computer and to have the addresses either printed out as stickers or print directly onto the envelopes themselves. The time and costs involved were reasonably high, so while more substantial companies could take advantage, small businesses did not use this approach as frequently.

The '90s ushered in email: a major game-changer. All a business had to do now was to ask the customer to provide an email address. They could send out as many messages as they wanted, as many times as they wanted, electronically. Small businesses were all over this because emails, of course, are free to send out. Even back when we were paying for Internet by the minute or the hour (it happened), it was still cheaper than using the postal service. It's important to note that in both of these scenarios, all of the customers received a touch point, or an impression, meaning that if the business sent something to 1000 people via snail mail or email, then 1000 people definitely received the message. It doesn't necessarily mean that every recipient opened or read the message (an engagement), but they at least had the opportunity to see it.

The 2000s brought us high-speed Internet, the beginning of the smart-phone era, and social media, primarily Facebook. Businesses no longer needed to ask customers for a mailing address or even an email address. Now, all they had to do was to get a customer to click a little button and "follow" their business digitally on a social media platform. Sending messages to customers through this medium made communication even more accessible and so, of course, messages became more and more frequent. Businesses could now send messages pretty much every day or even multiple times a day if they wanted to. Note that the same touchpoint applies here as it did before with mail or email. When you sent a message through Facebook to your followers, at least in the early days, they would definitely have at least an opportunity to see your post. However, as the site grew and grew, this became somewhat problematic for the social media giant.

In the early days of Facebook, everyone had the same page setup. Whether you wanted to be a person, a business, or a brand, you had the same options and the same delivery method. Somewhere in the mid-2000s, Facebook's customers, or users, started to complain, and some stopped using their service. Why? Because if I am following fifty members of my family and have two hundred more friends, then *that* is the reason I signed up: to see content from my friends and family. If I am also following fifty bands I like, thirty brands I love, and twenty-five organizations that I am fond of, I may not want to see their content as often. Unlike personal friends, many businesses and organizations usually have some form of a marketing department. So, when ten of the bands you like are all going on tour at the same time, their marketing departments will push pretty hard to get you to buy tickets and, in doing so, may be posting several times a day. Therefore, if you follow a lot of non-personal entities on Facebook in any capacity, and you're seeing every post that comes out, your Facebook feed is going to get jumbled really quickly. Enter the world of digital **spam** or overly advertised content that nobody wants. Facebook became a fountain of spam, and their users didn't like it.

In the early days of Facebook, advertising was only conducted by big companies who had to first make an appointment with a Facebook corporate salesperson and then shell out big dollars, or at least more than a small business could afford. So, Facebook got an idea and began to shift to a self-service advertising model. The first step was to differentiate between businesses/organization pages. Now, you had to pick a side: am I a person or am I a business/organization? It sounds simple enough, but this was a real game-changer, and this separation ushered in new tools for each entity to use, especially the businesses.

Another massive change was made at this time, which still has significant implications today, and many of you are probably not even aware of it. I'm talking about the Facebook algorithm concerning followers of your business. Most people use Facebook as a platform to keep in touch with people: that's pretty much it. While the other aspects are significant, most of Facebook's users are interested in getting content from their friends rather than from the businesses they follow. So because Facebook has now separated businesses and personal pages, all business content is shown to users far less often. While I still see *all* content from my friends and family, I will only see content from the businesses that I follow somewhere between 3-5% of the time, unless I decide to manually adjust this. That means that if you have 10,000 people following your business on Facebook, less than 500 of them will see this content appear on their feed organically. I'm not talking about engaging with the content; I'm talking about actually *seeing* it. This means that 9,500 people following your page *will never see your content.*

This change represents a significant shift in the customer relationship marketing model. Previously, all customers would receive *all* letters and emails sent to them. Now, however, posting something on Facebook does not guarantee that all of your followers will have the opportunity to see it. Reject denial; this is true for your business as well. Don't worry, though. There is still a way to make sure that all of the people following your Facebook page see your content: you pay for it.

After this change in algorithms, Facebook users began seeing far less commercial content, and small businesses were now able to advertise using some pretty nifty tools. Facebook–because they wanted to make a fortune, and who could blame them– created a self-service advertising platform that allowed businesses of any size to pay money to show their content (or ads) to as many people as they wanted, provided that they were willing to spend the money. Therefore, if you had 10,000 people following your Facebook page and you wanted to make sure at least 5,000 of those people would see your content, you'd have to pay for that. This is called **boosting posts.** Facebook also created a separate advertising platform called "Facebook Ads Manager" where you could target your audience more specifically and use a variety of functional options among other tools. Either way, Facebook had set up a way to allow any business, large or small, to advertise pretty much any content they wanted. All a business had to do was to simply spend the money required to push content to any user on their platform.

GETTING USERS WHAT THEY WANT

Let's switch gears for a minute and talk about search engine marketing. When you search for something on Google, you typically find what you want near the top of the page, if not in the first few options that follow. That's why Google became a juggernaut early on when compared to its search engine competitors such as Yahoo, Ask, or MSN etc. Google's search engine's job is, in its purest form, to give the user the content they want when they want it. Facebook is no different. The Facebook algorithm has a built-in aspect that will show the user content from businesses and organizations they prefer more often than ones they don't. Still, it will only do this if the user *tells* the algorithm that they want this content. How do they do that? By frequently engaging with a specific business's content.

Let's assume that Phil and Jill both like the brand Honda and are both following the business's corporate page on Facebook. Phil visits Honda's page a few times a week, looking for new cars and styles, while Jill just liked the page two years ago when she bought a Honda and never visited the page again. Phil, a user who shows Facebook that he *wants* this content, will be shown much more of this content than Jill, who has revealed that she's not interested, even though she's following the page. You could say that Honda's 3%-5% penetration on posts is 3%-5% *plus Phil*, as well as any other user who shows Facebook that they want this type of content by actively engaging. Therefore, if the organic (non-paid) or paid (ads) content that Honda puts out is frequently relevant and exciting enough for their target audience to engage with, Honda will move the algorithm in their favor. They are gaining a surplus of organic (free) penetration due to the frequency of users visiting their page and engaging with their content. These are the types of campaigns that you want: substantial engagement from users who are actively interacting with your content and visiting your page. It's also why you can have a ton of followers on Facebook but very little, if any, engagement. If this is the case, then you're probably just posting, not marketing. Successful brands on any social media platform know how to put out timely content that their audience is interested in and how to spend money where necessary in order to penetrate that audience, all the while working towards improving their organic reach through engaging content. That is how you run a successful social media site. Notice how I didn't say, "Tell everyone about your specials every day and post coupons and discounts twice a day." Why? Because nobody is interested in that, and that's where most of you are getting it wrong.

A massive push on the paid side (boosting ads or advertising) is, of course, a good thing too, especially for small businesses who now have a level playing field when it comes to marketing. In the past, if you wanted to create and market a new soda, you would have a tough time penetrating the marketplace due to the hundreds of millions of dollars spent by your competition on traditional advertising. Now, with social media functionality, you can connect with the same audience as Coca Cola and Pepsi. While a soda startup is most likely going to spend far fewer dollars and resources on marketing, they can still reach the same audience on the same platform. You can now have a successful little soda company, and if you have the right marketing and business strategy, you might be able to make it big. The one thing you must understand is that your marketing will not be successful just because you are doing something on a *new platform* or using something that *other people* have used to be successful. While luck is a real thing, and sometimes marketing works quickly with little to no effort, the majority of successful marketing campaigns are based on strategic planning and positioning that adjusts to market conditions. Social media is no different.

In the future chapters of this book, we're going to go through the complete marketing strategy for social media step by step, including budgeting and branding etc. It is essential to understand the concept of posts vs. ads, as you will have to decide how to use both of these in your social media marketing campaigns. Remember that posts are not any less valuable than ads and, in fact, they can be more useful if done correctly. And you do not always have to spend money to get your content out to your target audience. What you do need is an audience who is interested in your content and who can have the opportunity to interact with it. It can take time, energy, and money to build up, but think of this as rolling a little snowball down a hill. The farther it goes, the more snow it picks up, and the larger it gets. This is what you want. Sometimes, the best way to get your audience interested in your content is to put a small number of advertising dollars towards getting it going and then watch it bring you amazing results over time. The point here is to look at your social media as a customer relationship model and invest what is necessary to turn your stale old social media into a powerful marketing tool.

4

Key Strategic Approaches to Digital Marketing (or any kind of marketing, for that matter)

Marketing strategy starts with deep thought, common sense, and answering some fundamental questions. Before we dive deeper into the 5 Step system, I must first walk you through three classifications that will help you begin to think strategically about your product or business. Use these to determine the most effective way to position your business to your specific audience. The classifications are as follows:

1. **Jewelry or Groceries?**

2. **Branding or Call to Action?**

4. **Are You Searching For Them or Are They Searching For You?**

JEWELRY OR GROCERIES?

There are thousands, if not millions, of different products and services available in the world, yours being one of them. While I'm not one for restricting a business by putting it in a categorical box, I do find it helpful, in most cases, to guide business owners to look at their product or company from a 30,000-foot view. That is to say, take a step back and figure out what kind of product or service you are offering in relation to how people will perceive and interact with it. The first step in this process is to define your product or service as either jewelry or groceries.

When was the last time you walked by a jewelry store and they weren't having a sale? The answer, of course, is never. This is because jewelry is not something that most people purchase often. It is something that they buy a few times a year, at most, and usually for a special occasion. I am, of course, referring to expensive jewelry like a diamond ring, luxury watch, or birthstone accessory. These purchases are expensive, and they usually require time and energy in order to make an informed decision. Therefore, most people do not have an ongoing interest or need for information about this category of product. That's why most people walk by jewelry stores in the mall as if they have blinders on: because they do!

The opposite, of course, is true when someone is actually *shopping* for jewelry. Yesterday I wasn't interested, but I just remembered that my wedding anniversary is coming up next month, and now I need a diamond bracelet for my wife. Guess what, it's on sale! Wow! Like most people, I am only going to shell out that kind of money a few times a year, at most. Therefore, the jewelry store must always be having a sale, or else they may miss out on my dollars during those few weeks each year before my anniversary when I *am* interested. So, while it obviously makes sense for these stores to have sales at Christmas and Valentine's Day, having a sale all year long draws in the infrequent buyer who is seemingly taking advantage of a deal.

A "jewelry product" (or service), will be defined as an infrequent purchase that most people do not think about often, is only relevant in certain situations, and typically requires more effort and resources from the consumer than other products and services. Other examples include buying a car, planning a vacation, buying a new house, shopping for insurance, getting new furniture etc. Again, these are products and services that consumers are only interested in at specific times, usually only for short durations and for specific reasons.

Groceries, on the other hand, are everywhere. What I mean by groceries is anything pre-packaged and edible. These types of products are something that consumers think about often because everyone gets hungry. So, while you may only be able to get crumbled blue cheese at an actual grocery store, you can most likely buy a Coke, a Snickers bar, or a bag of peanuts at your local auto supply store while shopping for windshield wipers. It is also important to note that groceries are products that consumers, in most cases, *have to buy*. This kind of product is necessary for your lifestyle, although the specifics may vary depending on your social, cultural, or geographical location. Grocery-type product purchases are frequent, require small amounts of resources, and will most likely not require much time or energy to procure. Groceries are everywhere, everybody buys them, and everybody needs them.

Deciding whether your product or service is jewelry or groceries will help you to begin to understand the customer's perception and relation to your product or service. Remember that you need to apply this classification to the specific consumer of your unique product or service, which means that a small business owner might buy office supplies as a grocery product and business insurance as a jewelry product. Additionally, a dentist may buy dental chairs as a jewelry product and toothpaste as a grocery product. All consumer bases have products and services that they buy frequently and infrequently, and this will differ depending on the industry and specific audience you are trying to reach. Depending on how the consumer purchases and views your particular product or service will help you in shaping your messaging. This should aid in guiding the scope and balance of your overall marketing campaign.

BRANDING OR CALL-TO-ACTION

Think of two trains going down parallel tracks at the same time at the same speed. They will inevitably reach their destination at the same time. Now think of both of those trains splitting off into two different tracks, going different speeds, and traveling different distances, but ultimately arriving at the same destination. One is branding, and one is call-to-action, and both are equally essential marketing ideas.

Call-to-action is the train on the shorter track that arrives at the destination first. A call-to-action is something that you ask a consumer to do such as come to an event, purchase a new menu item, use a coupon, sign up for a rewards program, or follow you on Instagram. These types of marketing tactics are the primary means of getting your consumers to do something specific concerning your product or business. This type of marketing is essentially asking your consumer to take an action step that will ultimately lead them to an experience that will positively impact your business.

Branding, on the other hand, is the train on the longer track and while it, too, arrives at the desired destination, it takes a much longer and more complicated route to get there. Branding is how your customers perceive your business or product. It does not necessarily result in a direct call-to-action. What it will result in is the consumer's awareness of your product or company. They will use certain traits and characteristics to form an opinion about your product in their mind. This approach typically results in the consumer relating your product to similar experiences, which is sometimes referred to as a "Comp Set" (or competitive set). Branding typically has a longer lasting effect as compared to call-to-action, but it will take longer for the consumer to take any action because they have not been directed to do so.

Business owners often get these two concepts confused. They tend to think that by purchasing a paid article about their business in a local magazine, putting up a billboard for a few weeks, or posting a beautiful food item on their Instagram page, they will immediately see an increase in sales. This approach is unlikely to produce these kinds of results due to a lack of a call-to-action. It will, however, get more people to see your business in the light that you want them to and to consider the product, trade, or service in the future. In contrast, if you put a coupon in a local mailer, create a Facebook job posting, or put out a Snapchat Geofilter for your event, these will likely result in a more direct response from the consumer. Why? Quite simply because you are asking the consumer to do something: to participate in your call-to-action. Without the *ask*, you are most likely running a branding campaign, which can have a positive impact on your business but will not, and usually *cannot*, be measured in terms of a specific, tangible cause and effect. Therefore, you must understand what kind of marketing campaign you are running, or you may have unrealistic expectations that fail even before they begin.

Remember, though, that these two marketing ideas are not mutually exclusive. All marketing campaigns are branding campaigns, but they are still not necessarily call-to-action campaigns. That is to say, you cannot run a call-to-action campaign without running a branding campaign. Let's assume that you're running a marketing campaign for a high-end, fancy steak house, and your goal is to increase weekday traffic. If you put an offer on Groupon for 50% off and then share it with your Facebook followers, you have just created a sound call-to-action campaign. However, by doing so, you may not have taken into consideration the negative branding element you could have created. The fact that a high-end steakhouse is sharing a platform with other, more casual restaurants may lower the restaurant's perceived value, painting their brand in a desperate or lower-quality light. Or say that a salon owner places a Facebook Offer for 20% off for first-time customers; this is most likely an excellent call-to-action idea for the business. However, if the owner or marketer uses a low-quality picture for the creative content and spells a few words wrong in the copy, this will result in a negative branding impact on the consumer as the salon needs to be seen as a quality, detail-oriented business. So, while both companies may achieve short-term success with their call-to-action campaigns, they could experience long-term losses if their brand is perceived negatively in the process.

It is important to note that call-to-action campaigns are not more valuable than branding campaigns. Both are equally important in the scope of your overall marketing efforts and should work together by giving the consumer insight into *what you want them to think about when they think about your business or product.* If you were to lineup hundreds of your short-term call-to-action campaigns and take a step back to look at them as a whole, you should see a distinct picture of your brand. *Please note that I have devoted an entire chapter to branding later on in this book and will discuss this idea in much more detail. I will help you define what your brand is all about and how it will affect your digital marketing campaigns.*

ARE YOU SEARCHING FOR THEM OR ARE THEY SEARCHING FOR YOU?

There are two distinct approaches to digital marketing, stemming from how your product or service connects with and is perceived by the consumer. Some products or services are things that consumers search for, and some are things that consumers will find whether they search for them or not. Herein lies a crucial distinction that you must understand before beginning any digital marketing or social media marketing campaign. For example, if you develop a new Chicago-Cubs-themed ice cream bar, this is probably not a product that anyone is going to search for specifically. That doesn't mean, however, that this is a product no one wants to purchase. An item like this can be targeted to consumers who like the Chicago Cubs, ice cream, or who live in the Chicagoland area. Therefore, the Chicago Cubs Ice Cream Company is participating in the process of searching for consumers. The opposite scenario would be a car insurance company using a Chicago Cubs player as its spokesman. When someone needs car insurance, they will search for "car insurance" on various platforms. The Chicago Cubs player's image may be used to draw the consumer's attention during the search, but the consumer is actively already searching for the specific product or service.

Facebook, Instagram, and Twitter are massive "you're searching for them" examples, as marketers can draw from the interests and behaviors of consumers to place almost any product or service in front of them, no matter how silly or ridiculous. The more information a user enters, the more specific the advertising content can become. In contrast, Google is the big kahuna when it comes to "they're searching for you" content. These advertisements, of course, can refer to pretty much any product or service in the universe. It is important to note that certain types of products and services fit into these categories better than others. Facebook and Instagram, while mostly "business-to-consumer" driven, are becoming more "business-to-business" oriented. However, consumers are still going to be more likely to "Google" things that they need quickly, like a plumber; something requiring research, like real estate; or something that they don't understand, like medical advice. Consumers are also more likely to use Facebook, Instagram, or Twitter to search for the date on an upcoming concert, the latest fashion trends, or the menu of a particular restaurant.

Good marketers use these insights to create campaigns to lure consumers wherever they decide that they want them to go. You can run Google Ads for your flower shop when someone is searching for "prom bouquets" in your area, and then link them to your Instagram page to view what you have in your inventory. You could also run Facebook Ads to people who may fit the profile of someone interested in buying long term care insurance, put a pixel on your website, then follow them around the internet with ads as they are search for other things. According to our previous classification, jewelry products will tend to fall into "they're searching for you" situations more often than not, while grocery products will tend to fall into the "you're searching for them" classification. Then, depending on what kind of campaign you are running (be it branding or call-to-action), you can adjust your campaign to get someone to do whatever it is that you decide you need him or her to do. When you do this, congratulations, because you've just begun the process of building a marketing strategy for your campaign.

5

Defining Digital Marketing Goals

As a business, it is essential to define what, exactly, you intend to achieve through your digital marketing campaign. For many, the apparent goal might be driving more revenue, boosting sales, or attaining more leads. However, these goals are not necessarily the only reasons. I would argue that while driving more revenue should always be the goal of any good marketing program, the reality is, it's not always that simple.

Let's take, for example, the ultimate goal of a professional baseball team like the Boston Red Sox that, every year, aims to win the World Series. To do so, the Red Sox have to focus on several aspects of their team and their business. One of these aspects is hitting. They need to spend time and energy finding a hitting coach, allow ample time for hitting practice, and invest in hitting equipment. It is safe to say that a baseball team that doesn't hit well will most likely *not* win the World Series. It is also true, however, that a team that hits well won't necessarily *always* win the World Series every year either. Learning to hit well is one of many smaller goals that, together, contribute to the overarching goal of winning the World Series. Therefore, you could argue that *achieving superior hitting* is the team's goal specifically in relationship to hitting. My assumption is that, for many of you, digital marketing should be regarded as one aspect of your organization, just as hitting is one aspect of a successful baseball team.

Thanks in large part to the expansion of smartphones and mobile devices, social media has become a lifestyle: a modern and vastly popular lifestyle. It is so prevalent, in fact, that it is almost taboo for a company or business to *not* use social media in one form or another. Therefore, defining the goal of social media marketing can be a bit confusing at times. It may be a revenue driver for some and a necessary evil for others.

There are several different reasons for a business to invest in social media and digital marketing. You must first define a goal and, based on that chosen reason, you can then validate whether or not your campaign was successful. The six goals listed below are not the only possibilities, but based upon my years of experience, I believe that most of you will identify with least one. I want to help you define your goals, ways that you might be able to achieve them, and reasons *why* you have them in the first place.

1. Build Revenue

2. Drive Awareness

3. Lead Generation

4. Keep Up With Your Competitors

5. A Progressive Marketing Action

6. Not Sure

GOAL #1: BUILD REVENUE

The most popular reason that companies spend money on marketing is to create more money. This concept doesn't require much further explanation. Digital marketing is no different. If building more revenue is your goal, however, there are a few different ways to do it. All of the steps that I listed (except maybe #6), will help to build revenue in one form or another, but you need to decide if you're looking for direct or indirect revenue.

Direct revenue I will define as a marketing equation with a simple financial cause and effect. For example, if I sell digital watches, I might run an ad with a link that lures customers to click and purchase a digital watch. I sell X amount of digital watches as a result of spending Y amount of money on my digital advertising. **Indirect revenue** is revenue that that is not necessarily gained as a direct result of any specific marketing equation. For example, let's say I own a nail salon and decide to renovate the interior and add some new products and services in order to drive more revenue. Over a few weeks, I post pictures and videos of what my newly renovated salon looks like on various social media pages, which include new products and services. As a result of this, my sales increase 20% over the course of the year.

Each campaign resulted in increased revenue, but only the direct revenue campaign is a cut and dry marketing equation. The indirect campaign, while still profitable, is much more difficult to quantify, as it was the result of many different kinds of content, levels of advertising spending, and types of platforms. Neither type of campaign is more valuable than the other, but the direct marketing campaign will be much easier to scale and duplicate. While you can certainly scale and replicate the indirect campaign as well, you will need to spend much more time and energy figuring out which marketing efforts worked best as well as where, when, and how. So, it is essential to understand which of these approaches you are using in order to maintain realistic expectations.

GOAL #2: DRIVE AWARENESS

Social media is a fantastic outlet for drawing attention to just about any event, product, or business you can think of. The lighting fast delivery and seemingly endless amount of users to choose from makes digital marketing the go-to choice for getting eyeballs on your particular idea or marketing collateral. Remember, though, that the value of awareness cannot always be measured in sales revenue. There are times when marketers use awareness to promote products or businesses on social media that customers could not purchase even if they wanted to. This is known as a **supportive marketing campaign:** a non-revenue driving campaign used to support a revenue driving campaign.

Let's say, for example, that I am the marketing manager for a local park district, and we have just signed a deal to open a new pool in our community, but it will not open for twelve months. I can use this information to run very successful awareness campaigns on my social media channels centered around the new pool and my organization's brand. I am primarily running a *tease campaign*, or pieces of marketing used to build interest in a business or product. For the first six months, the digital marketing campaigns I execute for my new pool (that doesn't yet exist) will pull in very little, if any, actual revenue for my organization. I will, however, have the opportunity to engage with my target audience, create excitement about my brand, gain followers on social media, and get word about the new pool out to my community. Once we get closer to the pool opening, I will be able to switch gears and drive revenue by selling pool passes through the digital outlets I have spent time, energy, and resources building. Much of the positive revenue growth that is achieved in later months can, and should be, credited to the successful awareness campaign from earlier months. So, while revenue is always the goal of marketing, understanding how to measure a supportive campaign is an essential aspect to consider when setting goals.

GOAL #3: LEAD GENERATION

Social media marketing can become an extension of the sales department by generating leads. In these instances, potential customers will provide you with specific information about themselves—such as their name, phone number, or email address—via some kind of portal, and will then wait for you or someone in your company to follow up. Most social media platforms will have a lead generation function of some kind or another. Either way, you gain leads as a function of your call-to-action message.

Leads can be collected internally or externally. **Internal leads** are collected without users having to leave the platform. The social media platform collects their information and allows you access. **External leads** are collected outside of the social media platform. This is usually done via a landing page or website of some kind.

Lead generation can be a very powerful aspect of your digital marketing efforts and works well for companies with larger ticket (such as jewelry-type) products. Typically, justifying the need for detailed customer information requires more effort on the part of user, and will not usually be appropriate or effective for easy-to-access, grocery-type, products.

GOAL #4: KEEPING UP WITH YOUR COMPETITORS

As a marketing professional, I am often asked both really great and also really dumb questions. One of the most common questions I am asked is about how much money some companies spend on advertising. Usually, this topic is trendy around the Super Bowl. I was once asked why Budweiser spends $150 million a year on television advertising. My answer: because Miller spends $125 million. (The numbers are made up: I'm just trying to make a point.) This idea of keeping up with competition in the marketing world is a significant reason why some companies decide to do what they do and spend what they spend. Digital marketing is no different. One of the most effective pitches a salesperson can use on a company not currently using social media marketing is: everybody else is doing it, so if you aren't, you must be missing out. Many times, this is the only reason that some companies decide to go down the road of social media marketing in the first place. However, I would suggest not throwing your money away just to be able to say that you have something now that you didn't have before. Try to understand *how* your competition is using social media to be successful, and then find ways to compete. Remember, though, that the most effective metrics used to validate whether or not you are keeping up with your competition might *not* be sales or revenue: they may be digital analytics. These supportive, indirect marketing efforts can be used to drive revenue and positive branding elements for your business, either now or in the future.

For example, let's say Jonah's Ice Cream shop decides to start using social media because a new ice cream shop just opened up in town with a strong social media presence. Jonah's begins to use social media to build an audience and drive engagement. For the first six months, Jonah's is still far behind their competitors in terms of followers and engagement, but in month number seven, Jonah's stumbles upon some content that its audience loves. This new content begins to take on a life of its own. Jonah's now uses this in other areas of its marketing, which leads to driving more revenue for the business. In this case, Jonah's competed in the world of social media metrics against a competitor until the marketing tipped, so to speak, and provided the business with an opportunity to drive more revenue than they had before.

GOAL #5: A PROGRESSIVE MARKETING ACTION

While marketing hasn't changed, it certainly has evolved quite a bit over the years. For many of you, penetration into digital marketing is a result of keeping up with where your customers are and where they are not. If your company was previously advertising heavily in places like the yellow pages, you might be using social media as a replacement marketing tool. In any case, be sure to use similar metrics when evaluating your marketing strategies on non-digital platforms. While you may have to re-learn a few things (hopefully this book is helping you to do so!), the goals that you had for previous marketing efforts remain precisely the same, albeit revamped in newer, digital forms.

For example, let's say that you are the owner of a small plumbing company in a small town. For years, you have been advertising in the local newspaper for $300 per month, and this generated 3-5 new leads per month. Due to a shift in the modern landscape, the publication goes out of business. You now have no way to advertise to your community and, thus, you decide to enter the world of digital marketing. You decide to create a social media page and run a lead-generation campaign. You spend $300 per month, which is the same amount of money that you spent on print media. Now, you are generating 3-5 leads per month: the same amount of leads you were getting from the newspaper.

In this example, you can see that some businesses simply need to replace their traditional marketing with something more relevant to their audience's lifestyle. The marketing actions and platforms used are quite different, but the marketing equations remain the same. In these cases, your goals may not change at all, even though you are switching to digital marketing channels for the first time.

GOAL #6: NOT SURE

The unsure approach is *by far* the most common goal that businesses have when using social media and digital marketing for the first time. This includes some who studied marketing in school but were never taught the ins and outs of digital marketing and therefore don't know how it can be used to build successful marketing campaigns. If this is where you are coming from, I commend you for taking the time to get through the first five chapters of this book: something that may have been quite painful to read.

Books like the one you are reading (as well as many others) can and will help you to figure out just what you *should*, and in some cases *could*, do by running successful digital marketing campaigns. If this is you, then I'll ask you to spend a little more time reading through this chapter. Try to figure out what your specific goals are and continue reading this book until the end. In the next section, we will start getting practical as I will begin to walk you through the 5 Step process in its entirety.

6

Step #1 - Finding the Right Audience

Creating a marketing campaign without a specific audience is like someone giving you directions to their house without providing the address. You wouldn't know where to begin, where to go, or even whether or not you actually arrived. The process by which we begin all marketing campaigns starts with the idea that we are trying to reach a specific group of people and not just "everybody." Marketing campaigns that aim to reach everybody *can* be achieved, but typically they must be oriented around an idea, product, or business with strong universal appeal. I would urge you to stay away from marketing to everyone and, instead, to focus on creating targeted audiences.

Creating targeted audiences is not a new or novel idea, and marketers and business owners have been using this exercise for decades. In the previous world of traditional marketing, Neilson and other audience measuring companies created an entire industry around providing customer data to media buyers and planners about the types of people who are listening to or watching almost any form of media. Even billboards and outdoor advertising companies will provide you with a breakdown of the types of people who are most likely going to be driving by your advertisement during a specific time of day. So, while the ins and outs of how these companies come up with this information may be a bit more underwhelming then you'd expect, the modern digital platform as it relates to defining and reaching your audience has really changed the game. This is because data compiled in previous measurements was compiled by speculation or scientific estimation. Primarily, researchers would gather information about a small sample of people and then assume that these measurements would hold for the majority of a similar population. Companies would expect certain things about a person based upon their age, income, geographic area, etc. They would then take a small sample of users who listen or watch certain shows, for example, and create demographic assumptions based upon their findings.

Let's say a research company puts a special transmitter box on a 5% sample of TV watchers and logs their viewership time, channels, and shows. This information could then be used to create assumptions about all TV viewers in similar demographics and to provide advertisers with insights about where to best spend their money, depending upon their target audience. Don't get me wrong, this is not a corrupt system and, really, how else would you do it in a non-internet world? Lucky for us, modern digital platforms not only provide marketers much more specific information, but they also provide it to everyone and basically for free. How? Because the data used to measure the audience is no longer assumed: it is provided directly by the users themselves

The birth of MySpace (yes, MySpace) and a few other short-lived social media sites in the late '90s to early '00s began the era of freely-given demographic information. This evolution paved the way for companies like Facebook, Twitter, and the like to mine valuable user-provided data for marketers. Please note that there is no information or user data that cannot be accessed by both marketing "lay" people and full-on digital marketing professionals. It is essentially *how* you use it that matters. Understanding who your audience is, where your audience is, and what your audience is interested in will help you to create meaningful and relevant marketing campaigns that work. The study of this idea is so important and vast that it could easily be its own book. Maybe one day it will. However, I am going to break it down into a few categories that should help you to further define the right audience for your business or product.

1. Demographic

2. Geographic

3. Interests

4. Job Titles

5. Behaviors

7. Affiliations

DEMOGRAPHIC

The pitfalls of marketing begin to multiply when we don't focus on the basics. I have spoken to many business owners over the years who have complained that their marketing campaigns don't work, only to find that they have been trying to reach the completely wrong audience. So, as elementary and commonsensical as it may seem, *always* make sure that you understand the basic demographic information of your audience. This is critical. Demographic data is typically comprised of the following factors, as listed below. These factors will usually define your target audience on the most basic level.

a. Age

b. Gender

c. Income

As far as *age* and *gender* are concerned, some of this is pretty simple, but remember that, in many cases, you'll be marketing to multiple audiences at the same time. For example, if you are trying to sell prom dresses, then you probably want to reach an audience of 15 to 18-year-old girls (the user) as your *target audience*, or the specific group of people you intend to reach with your marketing collateral. Consider, though, that you have another, *secondary audience* of 40 to 55-year-old females: the users' mothers who are paying for the product. Without getting too far ahead of ourselves, stop for a second and think about the content that you would use to market to each audience: would it be the same or different? Would you use the same digital platforms for both, or would you use different ones? In this specific case, you may use Instagram and Snapchat to market to the target audience (15 to 18-year-old girls), and Facebook and Pinterest to market to the secondary audience (40 to 55-year-old females).

There is no limit as to how many audiences you can have for your digital marketing campaigns. Remember that each one will require you to go through the entire 5 Steps, as each should have a clearly defined audience, content created for that audience, budget, etc. In the case of prom dresses, we could add another audience of 40 to 55-year-old men, or the fathers of the users (15 to 18-year-old girls). You could add yet another audience to reach 12 to 14-year-old girls who are not going to prom this year but will be soon. Again, the same rules of running the 5 Steps would apply.

Income levels are also significant but typically assumed in the digital world. This is because while users may be very eager to share about their favorite bar or movie with friends and family, they are most likely not going to share how much money they made last year. What users may share, though, is where they live, their education level, and their job title. All of this information allows a digital platform to assume how much a person's income might be. We can, of course, do the same. For example, let's say that two towns sit next to each other. One has high property taxes, is mostly white-collar, and has a bustling downtown with high-end shops. The other is blue-collar, with smaller houses, and a simpler downtown with older businesses. While we can't put everyone into a box, which geography would you target if you planned to sell luxury cars?

GEOGRAPHIC

The physical location of your business (city, state, zip code, etc.) is only one small part used to determine the **geographic** range of your target audience. It actually has more to do with understanding your competition's geographic location than anything else. If you run a brick and mortar business, ask yourself this question: how far is someone willing to drive to my shop and, if they do, how many replacement businesses will they pass along the way? Google or Apple maps make finding this information a relatively straightforward process. Spend some time researching where your competition is located and what they offer.

Before we move on, I want to define a few terms for you. A **replacement business** is a similar business with similar offerings that could act as a replacement for your business in the consumer's mind. This is why you never see two Mexican restaurants open up right next to each other; they are replacement businesses for one another. Remember, too, that replacement businesses are all predicated on value. This is why some people may drive a little further to go to a salon that they prefer, for whatever reason, while passing three similar salons along the way. Replacement businesses can be a huge roadblock when it comes to successful marketing, and understanding how your business fits into the landscape of your specific industry will give you insight into determining a proper geographic range for your audience.

A **competitive advantage** is how your business competes in your industry or what you can offer the customer that your competition (replacement businesses) cannot. It may refer to one or many aspects of your business. It may be tangible, or it may not, but it is what separates you in the marketplace. Remember that some companies do not need a competitive advantage to be successful. Take the fast-food industry, for example: you will see the same type of restaurants, which are replacement businesses for each other, every couple of miles. These types of businesses are usually frequented by users who choose based upon personal preference rather than available products or branding elements.

As an example, let's say you are the marketing manager for a fun center: a birthday party place for kids with an arcade and such. You know that there are several similar or replacement businesses within 50 miles of your location. You now have to select what geographic area you want to penetrate with your advertising. Of course, you want to make sure that you are maximizing your exposure to the right audience. After doing some research, you feel that your competition is vast and that your competitive advantage is low. Because of this, you decide to limit the geographic range of your target audience to 10 miles surrounding your fun center. It appears to be the right move because your fun center is very similar to almost all of the other fun centers in the area. You choose to compete by reaching the audience with the shortest amount of distance to travel, or the path of least of resistance. Let's say, however, that as a result of this research, you decide to add a competitive advantage in the form of a rock climbing wall that none of the other fun centers in the area have. Now, you should increase your geographic marketing range based upon the fact that, while your competition may be high, so is your competitive advantage.

Let's also consider a massage parlor that has no replacement businesses nearby for 30 miles. In this case, the massage parlor should consider a geographic range of up to thirty miles because their customers have minimal choice in the market for this particular service. Sometimes, when businesses assess themselves against the nearest replacement business, they find that they can expand their geography even further. Let's say, for example, that after doing some research, the massage parlor finds that the nearest replacement business is a home-based business as opposed to a spa with ten massage therapists. Moreover, they find that the replacement business therapist is not much of a therapist after all and is just a non-licensed massage enthusiast who gives massages out of their home. In this case, the massage parlor may decide to not even consider the independent amateur a replacement business. They may need to continue their research and look more deeply into the market to find the nearest actual replacement business in order to further determine an appropriate geographic range for their campaign. Remember that the *value* of your product or service is the determining factor of how you define your audience, not the product itself. The marketing value is created by advertising and shapes your message in the mind of the consumer. While sometimes you may be able to reach more people by expanding your geographic area, you want to make sure you are not reaching many more of the *wrong* people.

Defining your audience using geography is also a way to limit your reach in order to get your product or service in front of the right people with the least amount of "loss" as possible. **Loss** is a marketing term used to refer to an audience who are exposed to your marketing but who most likely cannot, or will not, purchase your product. For example, let's say that you are the marketing manager for a restaurant chain that has fifteen identical restaurants in a large metropolitan area. After doing some research, you determine that the majority of your customers will drive no more than 10 miles to eat at your establishment. You are looking for ways to streamline your marketing, and you decide to look into radio advertising as a marketing platform. You determine that when advertising on the radio, you will have to purchase advertising that will reach the entire metropolitan area due to the broadcast frequency of the radio station. You determine that you will surely reach everyone within 10 miles of your restaurants (your target audience), but you'll also reach many other trade areas where people fall well out of your ten-mile radius. While you are reaching all of your local trade areas, you will have a significant "loss" of people who will be exposed to your marketing but who, according to your research, are most likely not going to be eating at your restaurant. Using digital marketing, you can now run campaigns targeted to a specific city, town, zip code, or even the ten-mile radius around fifteen different restaurants in a large metropolitan area. These buys result in very little, if any, loss and are a much more efficient and practical way to advertise.

INTERESTS

The availability of insight into user interests is one of the most fundamental, game-changing tools of the modern digital world. No longer do marketers need to make assumptions about their audience based on research. Consumers, now, actually *tell* us what they like and, in some cases, don't like. Marketers now have the opportunity to dive much deeper into specific, tangible interests of almost infinite possibility. The beauty of Facebook and what many social media sites did not understand early on, is that most people have narcissistic tendencies and want to share their likes and dislikes with anyone who will listen. Therefore, when millions of people started signing up for Facebook, a market of information was born. This market consists of people freely giving up virtually all of their personal preferences. Marketers were all over that.

For example, let's say you're promoting an Eagles cover band at a local music venue. Digital marketing makes it very easy to find the right audience for this event. You start by finding people who have told a digital platform that they like the Eagles. Next, you can dig deeper and find people who like Don Henley or Joe Walsh: members of the Eagles. You could expand this search further by finding fans of similar bands like Fleetwood Mac or Crosby, Stills, Nash, & Young. Then, using other factors we discussed—such as geography, age, or gender—you can create specific promotions for these users who are interested in the Eagles on at least some level. Plus, we know they live close enough to the venue to potentially buy tickets to the show.

The next step would be some fine-tuning to adjust to the size of the audience by considering the scope of the project. *Scope* is understanding the size of the marketing campaign in relation to the size of the product, service, or event. Are the Eagles cover band a local band, a national touring act, or the actual Eagles? Is the venue selling tickets, charging a cover, or is it a free show? Is this a weekend show or a weekday show? Is this is a large or small venue? All of these factors need to be taken into consideration when defining your audience. For example, the draw of a national touring act on a weekend night should be a much more substantial draw than a free show on a Tuesday night for a local band playing their first gig. Again, remember that the *value* of your product or service is the determining factor of how you define your audience, not the product itself.

Interestingly, because we can now essentially define the marketability of a product using digital audience metrics, the metrics can actually be used to determine the product. For example, I recall a concert promoter who once asked me who would be a better headliner for a night of live music at a specific venue: a Journey cover band or a ZZ Top cover band. I could have guessed, but first I searched on Facebook within a 25 mile radius surrounding the venue for a demographic age of 35 years or older, both men and women. What I found was that 87,000 people on Facebook liked Journey and 68,000 liked ZZ Top. So, I gave all of this information to the promoter, and they went ahead and booked the Journey cover band. By working backward, you can let the availability and size of the audience determine the product you bring to the market.

Interests are not limited to bands, movies, and television shows, however: they can be almost anything. On most social media sites you can define an audience based on multiple factors such as styles of music (rock, ska, jazz), type of cuisine (Italian, falafel, cheeseburgers), brands (Apple, Nike, Prada), famous people (Ricky Gervais, Albert Einstein, Hillary Clinton), book titles, characters, video games, religions, sports, ethnic cultures, and so on. Open up your mind, get creative, and find the interests of people who relate to your business. It's actually kind of fun!

Sometimes, there may be instances where you won't be able to find the interests of the audience you're looking for. In this case, you need to get creative. Think of an interest that might work if you were trying to define an audience of homeowners in a specific region. First, you might try "homeowners" or something similar. If that wasn't available, you might find something that would *define* the homeowners. How about Home Depot, DIY network, handyman blog, home improvements, or homeowner's insurance? Sure, there will be some loss, but you will still have an audience within a geographic area with the majority of an audience who are, you can assume, homeowners.

The size of an audience is also an important aspect to note. Most social media sites will tell you whether or not your audience is the right size for effective marketing. Compare this to a professional photographer who doesn't use the "auto" feature on his expensive camera. For a layperson, using the auto settings is a great choice, and it takes excellent pictures, but the professional who uses manual settings can create even better pictures. The point is to use your instincts when deciding if your audience is too large or too small. It all depends upon who you are trying to reach and why. As a rule of thumb, 100,000 people is the maximum size I would recommend for any small business to use as their audience. 50,000 to 75,000 usually works better. Anything larger than that often tells me that the audience is too broad, whether in interests, demographics, or geography. If this is the case, the best thing to do would be to re-work your audience a little bit to make it more manageable. In doing so, you'll make it much more effective and easier to manage.

Below is a list of examples of interests you could choose for your campaigns and ways in which you could break them down further with more specific targeting, if you needed to.

Broad Interests

1. Basketball

2. Republicans

3. Superheroes

4. Parents

5. Luxury Cars

Corresponding More Specific Interests

1. Basketball - Lebron James

2. Republicans - Tea Party Patriots

3. Superheroes - Lego Batman

4. Parents - Moms with Preschool Children

5. Luxury Cars - Tesla

JOB TITLES

Sometimes, you might want to market to a specific industry or professional field, and job titles are a great place to start. Just as users tell us what kind of music they like or their favorite vacation spot, they also tell us what they do for a living. You can break down an audience based on several factors related to job titles including the specific profession, industry type, or general field. You can define an audience of specifically electrical engineers or an audience of *just* engineers. The latter will be included in the group of the former, which will also include civil engineers, aviation engineers, and even LEGO engineers. Be sure to understand who you are trying to reach. If a broad audience is what you're going for, then you may want to select a group of users from an industry like hospitality, real estate, or health care. Remember that, when doing so, you are including everyone from this industry at varying levels. For example, everyone from a cashier, to a chef, to a restaurant owner could be included in the hospitality mix.

Be aware that most social media platforms do not provide users with a mandatory job title prefix selection. So, if I am a swimming coach, the only given option I may be able to select is "swimming instructor." This is not necessarily the same thing. Most sites will also let users write pretty much whatever they want if nothing provided suites them. In this case, I may consider myself the "head swimming coach" and enter this as my job title. Therefore, when you are trying to reach people who teach swimming, you may have several choices to pick from.

BEHAVIORS

Due to the digital nature of the current world marketplace, it seems that everything you do is tracked in one way or another, but good marketers like you can use data like this to ensure that you are reaching the right target audience. Social media and digital media companies are tracking you, whether you are on their platforms or not. **Re-marketing** is the reason why, when I go to ESPN.com and then to Facebook, I see ads for Monday Night Football on Facebook. This is because the majority of websites and social media companies are linked via pixels or digital codes that tracks the user when they leave a site and follows them around the internet. This way, digital media companies can make assumptions about your future behaviors based on the data they collect about you.

For example, if you go to Expedia.com and search for a vacation near a beach, you may end up seeing ads from Expedia about beach resorts on Facebook, but you may also be put on a list (so-to-speak) of someone who is "likely to go the beach." The behavior of "likely to go to the beach" is what we would define as a "behavior". This information may be very valuable to someone who sells vacation insurance, sunscreen, or bikinis. The same is true if you are searching for a new car on Cars.com. Based on your age and income level, which is assumed based on where you live and your occupation, you may be put on a list of someone who is "likely to buy a car in the next six months."

Facebook also tracks data from consumers who are most likely to click on ads, watch videos, and make online purchases. They know this because they track and rank peoples' tendencies to commit specific actions in the digital world. Therefore, when you put together a digital marketing strategy, you can use behaviors, along with other audience information, to nail down the perfect audience for your product or service. The only thing that you have to remember is that availability behaviors, and all potential audience data for that matter, change all the time. You may find an audience that you really like and then come back one day only to find they have removed some of the behaviors, or even interests, that you have been using. It's part of the game. Just remember that if they take some away, they have probably added others, and since you are a rockstar marketer, you'll be able to overcome.

AFFILIATIONS

Affiliations can be an incredibly powerful tool in the world of digital marketing. This is a deeper dive into the mind of your target audience. These are typically used when the majority of other choices to define your audience aren't present, don't seem to work, or else provide us with an audience that is either too big or too small. Affiliations are groups of people, publications, or associations that your target audience belongs to or follows.

For example, let's say that you are a golf course architect, and you want to reach an audience made up of golf course superintendents nationwide. You can start by searching for job titles (golf course superintendents, golf course greenkeepers, etc.), and you'll most likely find an array of professions that relate. After selecting these, you might find that your audience is too small to market to, and you'll need to find more users to fit into your target audience. What can you do? For one, you can search for affiliations like "Golf Course Superintendents of America," the national association to which your target audience is most likely to belong. Sure there will be some people who follow the "Golf Course Superintendents of America" who end up just being casual fans of golf, but not likely. People who are a member of, or who follow, this organization are more likely to be industry professionals and not just your average Tiger Woods fan. Groups like this are everywhere, and you'd be surprised just how many groups have their own industry magazine, conferences, and online resources.

As far as affiliations go, Twitter is the go-to source. Due to Twitter's open policy on audience lists, you can target people who are following a specific page, which could be anything. For example, if you're promoting a concert for a lesser-known musical act with a decent social media following, simply define your audience as Twitter followers of the band's page who live within about 25 miles of the venue, and you're all set! You can do the same with any Twitter handle such as a magazine, brand, similar business, sports team, etc.

Facebook is a little different in that they (Facebook) have to provide you the option of affiliating with an entity on their advertising platform in order for you to use it. So while "The Pez Lovers of America" is an actual organization with a Facebook page, they are probably not big enough to be included in Facebook's choices when defining your audience. How do they decide which are allowed and which are not? Nobody really knows, but obviously the size of the group and the number of followers has a lot to do with it. You'll just have to do a search and cross your fingers!

Cross-platform affiliations are probably the most interesting and also the most infrequently used option when defining a target audience. It's a way to use contacts from another source by uploading them to a new source. For example, you could download all of the email addresses of your LinkedIn followers and upload them to Facebook. You can then have an audience on Facebook of people defined as your "LinkedIn Followers." You could buy a list of dental hygienists from an industry conference and upload those email addresses to Facebook as well. In either case, Facebook will search to see how many current users are affiliated with the email addresses you upload, and then you can put them on a list. In this way, you can take the contact information affiliated with one source and use it on another source to create a new target audience.

Hopefully, this has given you a lot to think about when it comes to defining your target audience. It's important to mention that most businesses and brands will have multiple audiences that they are marketing to at any given time. From here, we'll dive into what kind of content we should create for our marketing campaigns in order to penetrate our audience. Just remember to always start here first, no matter the temptation to jump to content creation. Always take the time to define your audience, as this is the cornerstone of all successful marketing strategies.

7

Step #2 - Create the Right Content

C ontent is a crucial part of the marketing machine. It is the most visible part of the process and, therefore, can influence the consumer in a major way, either for better or for worse. The content that you share with the world is a direct reflection of your brand, and this cannot be understated. Remember, too, that this content will not just be interpreted through your eyes but, possibly, by millions of other people's eyes, all with different lenses. Consequently, this step requires great caution. In this chapter, I am going to answer the three most important and most frequently asked questions that I get when it comes to posting content on your social media pages. Bear with me, though, because I think that this may be the most frustrating part of the process. Why? Because I cannot actually give you direct answers to these questions. I can't actually tell you what to do. All I *can* do is to point you in the direction of understanding the concepts, and then allow you to apply this knowledge to your specific business or brand.

For starters, there are hundreds of different kinds of content that you could use for your digital marketing campaigns, ranging from pictures and graphics to live video to geo-targeting filters. These, and other forms of digital media, are all great pieces of content to use, but before we move forward, let's get one thing straight. *Please* don't ask me, or anyone else for that matter, which pieces of content are the most effective or the most important. The answer to this question is, frankly, that all forms of digital content are equally important to the extent that they fit into a strategic marketing campaign. Remember, we are not just *posting*, we are *marketing*, and in doing so, we will use various forms of content to influence people to do what we want them to do. Thus, the sum of your campaigns is more valuable, in actuality, than each individual piece. Because as you use different forms of content correctly, you will begin to see that some perform better than others. The pieces that don't work well, however, help to guide us to the correct path and thus provide value in and of themselves.

For example, let's say that you are promoting for a standup comic at a comedy club. For most of the campaign, you have been busy posting pictures of the comic and the venue. You've also created graphics to communicate that you are hosting "comedy night" at a particular day and time. The campaign seems to be doing well, but then you stumble upon a 5 minute clip of the comic performing on YouTube. You find a 30 second portion which you feel will resonate with your audience. You cut out the 30 second clip and post it to Facebook and Instagram. Soon after, you begin to receive 10 times more engagement as compared to the static images you posted before. To build on this momentum, you cut another 30 second clip of the comic out of the same performance and post that as well. After a few hundred views of the second clip, some of your fans find what the comic is saying to be offensive and decide to boycott the show. So, while I (or anyone else) could have advised you that video will, in general, be a better choice than a static image to promote this show, it all depends upon the actual, specific video content itself. This example proves why each marketing campaign needs to be vetted based upon the actual available content. The value of great content is only relevant as far as its availability to a marketer in the first place, and the success of that strategy will always be judged based on the entire campaign, and not just one individual piece.

Varied content is a topic that will be further defined in Chapter 9 (Promote Your Business As A Brand), but it needs to be talked about a bit here before we go on. One of the most detrimental things you can do to on your social media pages is to post the same content (or the same kinds of content) repeatedly. Meaning, if all a restaurant does is post pictures of food, they are limiting their brand and creating a situation where some users will un-follow their pages due to overly repetitive content. Of course there are exceptions to every rule, but the majority of people are looking to interact with your *brand* on social media, not just your business. A brand is a living, breathing thing (so to speak), with many layers that need to be communicated. Food is typically only one aspect of a restaurant's brand, and elements like service, atmosphere, and community need to be brought forward as well in order to tell a complete story. The same is true for your digital marketing campaigns.

Next, I am going to get into the meat of what it means to post great content on your social media pages, and I will do so by exploring three questions that I am asked all of the time. Hopefully, these are questions you might be pondering as well. As we examine each one, consider how these might be relevant to your particular business or brand.

QUESTION #1: HOW MANY TIMES A DAY SHOULD I POST ON MY SOCIAL MEDIA SITES?

To answer this, let's start by defining a musical-turned-marketing term called **cadence**. Musically speaking, a cadence is a rhythmic flow: the basic movement that a musical composition follows. The same is true for digital marketing; you need to determine the rhythmic flow. This cadence is ultimately the measurement of how your audience interacts with and responds to your content. It is based upon the type of material posted and frequency with which that material is presented to the user. You need to try different amounts and different kinds of content, with varying levels of both call-to-action and branding elements, until you figure out what your audience responds to best. Then, exploit and build upon that.

For example, let's compare two businesses. One is a music venue that has live music 5 *nights* a week. The other is a music store that offers music classes 5 *days* a week. Without knowing anything else about the businesses, which do you think would be appropriate posting 3 to 5 times per day on their social media pages? The music venue, of course. Why? Because 5 different live events each week mean lots of bands and artists all performing at different times. This creates lots of content and multiple call-to-action steps such as dates, times, tickets, etc. Therefore, it is a reasonably unstructured marketing situation. A music store's class schedule, however, will probably only change a few times a year, and will most likely offer the same kinds of classes and teachers on a seasonal basis, resulting a reasonably structured environment. So, for the music store, posting three to five times per week is probably more than enough, and three to five times per day might be overdoing it a bit.

Businesses that are structured, predictable, and easy to access require fewer touch-points to the consumer in order to make an impact. The reverse is true for unstructured, **cold brands or businesses**. A cold brand or business is one of which most consumers, or target audience, have very little to no prior knowledge. This brand or business will require more frequent communication than a well-known competitor. A fancy way of saying this is that things that are new or complicated require more time to market than things that are older and simple. While this might be a commonsense concept, you'd be surprised how many social media accounts I have seen over the years where people are posting way too much or *way* too little. How do we know which is the right approach for your business? We measure it, of course, with a little tool called *engagement*.

Engagement is the action of someone taking an interest in your social media posts. Quite simply, they have to *do* something in order to interact with your content. This interaction differs from an **impression**, in which the content simply appears to a passive user. It is possible to have lots of impressions but very little engagement and vice versa. The measurement of an impression is typically universal in social media, simply meaning that the content has appeared to a user in some capacity. Engagement, however, can vary depending on the platform. Most platforms will measure likes, clicks, shares, and comments as engagement, while others will measure video views, or check-ins. Either way, the goal is to show the right content to the right audience so that they will engage with that content, resulting in either positive branding or call-to-action step.

The cadence of posting should become apparent once you have found a series of posts that provide consistent positive engagement with your target audience. In other words, determine the pattern with which you are showing content to your audience and whether or not they respond with lots of engagement. Typically, you'll know you're posting too much when you see very little engagement spread over multiple posts, and you'll know you're not posting enough when you see robust engagement on isolated posts. The best way to figure this out is to use a little bit of the scientific method we talked about earlier. Make a simple chart with the number of posts you had for the week, the amount of money you spent, and the total number of engagements you received. If you track this every week, you'll begin to see patterns. Another way to find your cadence is by monitoring the followers of your page. Track the total number of followers, new followers, and negative followers on your chart as well, and see if you can find a correlation between the number of posts and the total amount of engagement you receive. Remember that while this may seem like a little bit of hard work, it is far from complicated.

You must also consider the timing of your posts, as they reflect the type of business you have. If you are a breakfast restaurant open from 5:00 am to 3:00 pm every day, then it won't make much sense to post at 5:30 pm. If you are trying to get people to come to your event, be sure to start three weeks out, gradually building interest. Don't post for the first time the day before and expect significant results. If you're a bank or a simple nine-to-five business, then post sometime during the business day and maybe even track the times of the day you are posting on your engagement chart as well. Again, find a correlation with positive engagement, then exploit and build on that.

QUESTION #2: WHAT KIND OF CONTENT SHOULD I POST?

This is the million-dollar question, but I'll answer it. You should post content that communicates your brand and achieves a high amount of engagement with your target audience. It's a complicated question with a simple answer. It's even more complicated to execute. There is no right or wrong here, and this is the principal trial and error portion of the marketing process. For example, let's say you are the marketing manager for a company that sells high-end cosmetics, and your competitive advantage is that you donate to environmental causes with every purchase. Your content choices are seemingly endless, but let's discuss a few ideas for you and your company, all the while considering the branding and call-to-action element of each.

1. High-quality pictures taken in a studio, showing off the elegant package design; link to your online store.

2. Lower quality (cell phone) pictures taken by a customer who has just purchased the item at a local department store and is so excited; link to customer's Instagram page.

3. A minimalist graphic with a simple message, 3 to 4 words, having to do with the environment and just your logo below; no link.

4. High-quality video (less than 60 seconds) with famous models applying your product, then talking about how much they appreciate the philanthropic aspect of the business; link to your online store.

5. Low-quality (cell phone) video (2 minutes) of one of your company executives talking to an environmental activist at a significant, organized, and highly publicized industry event, but just having coffee; link to the activist's web site.

6. Pictures or videos of customers recycling or throwing away your competitors' products (which can damage the environment when manufactured), then a picture or video of the customer purchasing your environmentally friendly products, posted using your contest hashtag; everyone that does this in the next thirty days will be entered to win a $1000 gift card; link to the contest page with more information.

7. Ask, "What lipstick color do you feel like today?" with a graphic of only wording and nothing else; no link.

8. Join one closed environmental social media group, post and respond to at least three users every week; don't mention your specific products for at least three months; link as necessary.

There is obviously more to this than that but, hopefully, you can see that all of these content ideas are at least good enough to try. It would be hard to argue which of these ideas is the best but, as good as they might be, they would get old pretty quickly if we picked only one and just kept using it over and over again. The point here is that if you executed all of these as a strategic campaign over time, you would be effectively communicating your brand. Your audience would be engaging with your content on varying levels, and if you were tracking this (or using the scientific method), you would begin to see a pattern. Once you know the pattern, you can then start to exploit it, knowing what content your audience is most likely to engage with and when. Remember, too, that these ideas will not necessarily work for every business or organization. These ideas have been well thought out for this particular case, with an emphasis on taking into consideration a target audience. Let's take a closer look at these content categories and how they might help your specific digital marketing strategy.

IMAGES, GRAPHICS, AND WORDING

Images with wording are the most basic form of social media. Pictures are, indeed, worth a thousand words. They are an excellent way for you to communicate your brand or business without the user having to try very hard. It's sort of the difference between how many people will read a book versus how many will go see the movie version. There are fewer details in the film, and some of it may not be precisely what the author was going for, but the movie appeals to more people, is a medium more people are used to, and takes less amount of time and energy to digest. The same is true with pictures and visual media; more people are going to interact with images or moving pictures rather than just words on a screen.

The **80/20 rule** states that only 20% of people are going to read anything on your social media pages anyway. The majority will, however, quickly interpret the visuals on the page and come to some conclusion based on what they see. Visually speaking, what you show your audience is typically more important than what you say. It's why some social media posts are merely a graphic of text. Why? Because if you write the same wording in the text portion of Facebook and post it, not as many people will typically read it. As a graphic, however, that same wording will have a much better chance of getting noticed or creating some positive engagement.

Using pictures effectively is an art, and you must understand your end game: the point of what you are posting and the reason why. There is nothing wrong with posting low-quality images, but don't post them all the time. If a restaurant posts pictures of their food, then these should be high-quality images to make a high-quality impact. They can, however, still make a high-quality impact using low-quality images of food if the photo has another purpose. If a little league baseball team comes in, holds up their pizza slices, and you capture it with your cell phone in a bad lighting situation, this could be a great social media post that may drive lots of engagement. If, however, you are trying to visually show off the quality of your food, you need to use a good camera with good lighting.

If every picture has a purpose, then be sure to get to the point quickly, visually speaking. This means that if your image of the little league baseball team is taken from far away and there is a lot of dead atmospheric space in the shot, you should crop it so the user will focus on what you want them to see. Doing so makes it easy for the user to determine what you are going for. This concept works well for most pictures, so be sure to consider cropping any photo to ensure that the focus is crystal clear. The only time you don't have to worry about this is if you are taking and posting live pictures in real-time, or if you have lots of photos, such as in an album. I would still caution you against posting anything before editing. Remember, the only time you should ever break a rule is if you are doing it intentionally.

Uncropped   **Cropped**

The purpose of this picture is to highlight the two runners shown in the cropped photo. If the photo is not cropped, the viewer does not know where they are supposed to look.

Image quality is very important to take into consideration. Without getting too technical, all images have a certain level of quality depending upon the size and number of pixels. Be sure that any post you publish to your social media pages is a high-quality image or one that is not, in any way, blurry. You'd be surprised how many times I see blurry pictures on businesses' social media pages, and they look terrible. These kinds of images are typically found on holidays when everyone is searching for a "Happy Whatever" graphic and just using whatever they can find. Marketers that don't know any better (not *you*, of course!) will grab an image that looks good in a search preview but looks terrible on their social media. The rule of thumb is, you can make higher-quality pictures smaller, but you can't make low-quality images bigger.

Remember, too, that if you post a low-quality image on your phone and it looks ok, it is going to look very different when it is blown up on someone's computer screen. The best way to ensure that your photos and graphics look good is to post them on a computer or a tablet with a larger screen and then view them on your phone. Always be sure that you're going from large to small. You might also consider using photo-editing software of some kind to edit your pictures before you post them. You'd be surprised how easy it is with even very basic photo-editing software to turn a mediocre image a great one in just a few minutes. Remember that anything you post is a direct reflection of your brand, in one form or another, and you have to be intentional about it.

Clear Graphic

Blurry Graphic

There are other pictures you can use besides the ones you take yourself or pay a photographer to shoot. These are called stock pictures. I would caution you in using these, however, as they are typically a much better fit for a graphic or as a manipulated image of some kind. Using stock pictures as your own pictures is very obvious to most people due to their overproduced nature. Also, be cautious when sourcing stock pictures, as one of the mortal sins of the creative world is posting a stock picture with a **watermark**. A watermark is a transparent graphic embedded in stock pictures which can only be removed when it is purchased from the source. If you search Google for an image that you want to use, first be sure that it is not copyrighted, and then check to be sure that it is not watermarked. I have seen watermarked graphics posted to businesses' social media pages; nothing gives off more a clueless and cheap vibe.

Stock Picture of Family   **Stock Picture of Family
                                        with Watermark**

Graphics go hand-in-hand with pictures. They are a great way to visually communicate your ideas with images, letters, numbers, or symbols. Remember to create graphics for each specific medium. A graphic made for your Facebook page may not be the right size to fit on your Instagram page and vice versa. Creating graphics is not very complicated anymore, and there are some excellent photo-editing software suites out there, so don't feel you have to be a certified graphic designer to get this done;

you don't. With the right intention, even some basic, older publishing or photo-editing software suites can get the job done. There are, however, a few tricks of the trade that will separate a quality graphic from the rest. If you have the resources to hire a graphic designer, you might not necessarily need to know some of these tricks, but understanding the "why" will still be valuable to you.

Sample Graphics

Transparent images are something you'll want to wrap your head around if you haven't already. Transparent means that the image or logo you want to use doesn't have any background. Basically, it looks "cut-out."

Many times, companies put their logo on an image in a "box" on top of another image. This looks unprofessional. Photoshop or a similar program can do this easily, but there are many websites out there which will take your logo (or even pictures, in some cases) and make a transparent version for free. Figuring out how to do this can be a real game-changer.

Non-Transparent Logo **Transparent Logo**

The importance of creating specific graphics for specific mediums cannot be understated. If you have a marketing campaign running across multiple platforms, then you need multiple versions of the graphics you are using to fit each of the different platforms. Flyers are flyers, tickets are tickets, Facebook event header images are Facebook event header images, and so on. Don't try to use one or two sizes to fit them all; it won't work. So, while there are times when you'll have the benefit of double-dipping an image, so to speak, the majority of the time, each image needs to be created for a specific purpose or function.

Simple graphics are also usually the way to go. An event flyer posted at your local Starbucks often looks jumbled and has a ton of information (dates, times, website, etc.) because it only has a small space in which to communicate lots of information. There is no way for the user to further interact with the event flyer, though, nor is there any way for the flyer to actively link the user anywhere else in order to get more information. Social media posts have the luxury of doing all those things. So don't feel like you need to try to put all of the information about the event in the graphic itself or even in the wording box. Keep it simple, short, and to the point. Then, link the user to where they can get more information or details. A Facebook event page is a great resource to use for detailed information about your event. So is your website or even a **landing page**.

A landing page is a single-page website that has one specific purpose. Typically, it does not link to any other source. Landing pages are great if you want to collect consumers' information or give details about a particular product or event. You can create landing pages as independent sites or as part of your website (i.e. www.relevantelephant.net/holidayoffer).

Be sure that the page is designed with the idea of **conversion** in mind and nothing else. Conversion is the execution of a requested call-to-action. If you are running ads for consumers to enter a contest to win a $50 gift card, then your conversion is the number of email addresses you collect and nothing more. The landing page needs to be explicitly designed to collect email addresses, all the while communicating your brand, and that's all. Many times, marketers want to put more information on a landing page than is necessary.

Remember, too, that what you market to a consumer on social media should be exactly what you give them when they click on your ad or post. Therefore, if you are a company that provides roofing, siding, and window services and you are running ads for a window special, your landing page should be about windows. Not roofing. Not siding. Resist the temptation to put more information than necessary when that little voice in your head says *but our business does more than that!* I know it does, but then you need to create three separate landing pages, one for each product. If you're marketing all three products (windows, roofing, siding) at the same time, a general landing page with all three services is probably fine. It all depends upon the message you are presenting to the user and your explicit call-to-action. Short and sweet is also suitable for the wording in your post that accompanies a graphic or a photo. Using **shortened links** will help by reducing the length of some long URL links. This makes them easier for users' eyes to digest. There are many free online tools that will shorten links for you in about two seconds, so be sure to take advantage of these services.

Long URL

https://www.eventbrite.com/e/loft-28-west-wedding-fair-tickets-87250762379?fbclid=IwAR3B7mKc3-S7wN2h0ajCBwQCinrAobuYtiwi_NKLbsCpcUHg67D2Kopg4Hg

Shortened URL

https://tinyurl.com/tcn93mc

Knowing when to use a photo or a graphic typically depends on what creative collateral you have at your disposal. If you have some great pictures of your theme park, then putting your logo in the corner and posting a few from time to time with related wording makes sense. If you don't have great pictures or don't have any pictures at all, then you might need to use a stock graphic of a family looking like they're having the time of their lives. Add a snappy tagline and your logo, and you've got a great post. Either of these will probably work well, with the overarching decision based on the goal of the campaign and the availability of the content.

In a perfect world, one would have access to great high-quality pictures, great low-quality pictures, a killer variety of graphics, landing pages, banding steps, and a clear call-to-action. When that's the case, you can efficiently market to multiple audiences within the same campaign using different mediums. For example, let's say you're marketing a live, interactive dinner theater based on an 80's television show (why not?), and you have some great pictures from a recent performance showing off the '80s nostalgia. You might want to create an "'80s pop-culture based audience" using lots of specific interests and then post the pictures along with the logo of the show. Next, put the necessary information in the wording, written in '80s lingo (like "gnarly") and link users to the Eventbrite page for further details and ticket purchases.

If you also want to market to an audience interested only in dinner theater, those folks might not care about all of the campy throwback material. So next, you want to define an audience that is interested in "dinner theater" and "live theater" in general, again using interests. Next, create a graphic that conveys the concept of dinner theater, but not necessarily the 80's theme. Then, write the copy straight up while citing other famous, interactive dinner theater experiences that your show could be compared to (ones the target audience may be familiar with), and link them to the same Eventbrite landing page. Here you have one platform, two different audiences, and two different creative campaigns. But, you have the same landing page, event, and call to action.

Text-only posts should be used sparingly. You will almost always get more bang for your buck posting a visual with your wording. The exception, of course, is Twitter, which you could view as a mini-blog where you are continually sharing your thoughts. If that is the case, Twitter is an excellent medium. The rest of the social media platforms are usually dependent upon some form of a visual medium, accompanied by a short text and a clearly defined call-to-action step when necessary.

Another type of creative content to use, sort of a cross between text and image, is the emoji. **Emojis** are pictures in the format of text that convey a feeling, meaning, or idea. Emojis are used in the wording box of social media sites and are typically used to make a point or draw attention to something. Most social media sites will have a library of emojis already built-in in one form or another: anything ranging from smiling faces to a slice of pizza, the Mexican flag, or a Christmas tree. If you don't find the one you want, don't worry, because there are websites with catalogs of emojis that can be easily copied and pasted from one site to another. Emojis are a great way to enhance a post or shorten wording in order to help get your point across more quickly and efficiently. While widely used, emojis are not present in all social media posts, so they can help to make your post stand out from the rest.

Hashtags are a way for users to search within social media sites and find a specific topic of conversation or buzzword. A hashtag is a # in front of a word or phrase like #Christmas, #MondayMotivation, or #ChicagoBulls. There is no regulation of hashtags, so feel free to use as many as you'd like or even create new ones. Be sure to first understand how hashtags are used on the social media platform you are working on. On some social media sites, it is common and widely accepted to have several hashtags within a post. Specific platforms are set up for users to search using hashtags, so the tags are intentional and help the user find the content they are seeking. Other social media sites do not use hashtags as search engines as frequently, and if you post too many hashtags within your post it will look unprofessional.

Be sure to understand how hashtags work within the social media site you are using before you post or else you can come off looking clueless. Just as you need to adjust the size and layout of your graphics and images when crossposting, the same is true for your wording. Each form of social media has its own language, and you'll need to understand how each works if you decide to crosspost. In some cases, you may use the same wording from one site to another, but there are other cases where you will be limited and will need to troubleshoot in order to get your point across.

PRODUCED & NON-PRODUCED VIDEO

Videos are a great way to go beyond static mediums and tell a story. There are several different ways to use videos on your social media pages at varying levels of production. I would consider a **produced video** as one where you have a videographer or a professional camera, lights, sound, and a fully edited and finished product. It looks basically like a commercial like you might see on TV and, of course, the quality level can vary, depending upon how many resources you want to use. Remember, the '00s brought us into a stage of technology that gave almost anyone the ability to make high-quality video at a fraction of what they would have cost in the '80s or '90s. It's true, professional videographers are typically always going to give you a much better product than a video "layperson," but that shouldn't stop you from trying.

There are two major categories to choose from when executing a produced video of any kind: controlled and uncontrolled. A **controlled video** is where you have complete control over the environment. This is usually done when a business is closed or empty or is done off-site somewhere. Controlled shoots allow you to set up lights, adjust audio levels, move tables and equipment around, and interview lots of different people. It allows virtually complete control of your situation. **Uncontrolled video** shoots can still be done by a high-level videographer, but these occur in situations where your business is operating, or your event is happening. Good videographers will be able to adjust the lighting via their camera, but they will have less control due to the energetic atmosphere of the environment. Many times, a hybrid of these two styles works best as you can come in early before your shop opens and interview the owner, then come back and shoot some more when your store is open and has customers. You can then edit the two together.

The uncontrolled footage is referred to as b-roll. **B-roll** is generic footage is used on the screen to highlight something, or to be used as a backdrop while someone is talking. It helps makes videos more attractive to the viewer than watching a talking head on the screen for two minutes. B-roll works best when it is synced up with whatever is being said by the person doing the talking. If someone in the video is talking about their new espresso machine and how it works, then have some shots of the espresso machine in action while they're talking.

When producing a video for your social media page, you need to consider the scope: the amount of resources you need to use for the product, service, or event. If you are producing a video that you will show to an audience for only a week or two, you want to spend less money on resources than you would for a video that you'd be using for a year or two.

Let's say you are a family farm that caters to tourists but also hosts barn weddings. If you are going to produce a video showing this year's pumpkin harvest, you probably want it done well, and will use it as a commercial or promotion for a couple of weeks during the fall season. This project may require a professional videographer for a couple of hours. If you're producing a video to show off your wedding venue, then you probably want to use many more resources. As the wedding video will most likely be used for a year or two, it will probably require one or two professional videographers for at least a few days. If you just wanted to show off some knick-knacks you have on sale in your general store for the day, using bare-bones resources would probably be a good idea. You could get this done without hiring a professional and using your own mobile device and posting it for just one day. So, you have three different kinds of videos, all at varying levels of scope. This information should be taken into consideration when deciding how much money to spend.

The modern age that we live in should allow you to create video content for your social media pages almost as easily as static content. Remember that your marketing campaigns should incorporate all different forms of content including high-quality, low-quality, and even live video. Remember, the 80/20 rule that states only 20% of the people are going to read anything that they see your pages, so consider this when deciding if making a video is a good idea or not.

If your restaurant is offering a drink special on Tuesday night, then you might not need to spend resources making a video. A beautiful photo of the drink and a few graphics might do the trick. If your restaurant is changing and rolling out an entirely new menu, you might want to go with a produced video as your primary source of communication. Why? Because you now have to find a way to communicate lots of details (such as all the new menu items) as well as the "why" of the story (why you changed your menu) in a short, clear, and concise manner. So, while you can take a photo of each new menu item and use text to write why you're changing your menu, this will most likely result in a lot of pictures and a lot of words: something you could probably communicate much more efficiently in a one to two minute video.

You want to keep your photos cropped, graphics simple and wording short, and videos are no different. Typically, under two minutes is the rule, under one minute is the goal, and if you can get it done in 30 seconds or less, then god bless you. People have very short attention spans (I can't believe you are still reading this book!), so get to the point quickly. As each video needs to be short, it also should focus on one idea. I said *one idea per video!* That little voice in your head is going to creep up again and say, *but I also want to say this, and I also need to say that!* Fight it. If you have multiple ideas that need to be communicated, then create multiple videos. Sometimes, it's as easy as creating one longer video and then breaking it up into different segments. Remember, your audience cannot handle more than one or two ideas at a time, so keep it simple and keep it visual.

Low-quality video or **non-produced videos** can also be handy marketing tools. Cell phone video will typically be the preferred choice here. Though many modern phones have fantastic quality, I am referring to videos that are not set up with lighting, advanced audio recording, etc. These types of videos give the viewer the feeling of what's happening at your business in real-time. If you want to show off a big event that's going on, you could have a videographer come out and shoot it, and that's great, but a raw cell phone video can provide an exciting and unique perspective. If you are running a neighborhood sports bar and you want to show lots of people gathered at your place watching the big game, the low-quality video will most likely capture this feeling element better than a produced video. Why? Because a significant part of a neighborhood sports bar's brand should be the "local vibe," which is typically real and raw. Remember, though, that if all you *ever* post is raw, low-quality video, then you could be giving off a branding element of "low quality," which would most likely go against brand standards for just about any business.

LIVE VIDEO

These types of videos go hand-in-hand with *live video,* whereby you are broadcasting in real-time. The two major categories of videos apply here as well: controlled and uncontrolled. Uncontrolled live video shoots show off what is going on in your world right now: real and raw. For many of you, this will create a "see what you're missing" situation by making your audience aware of something they may have missed. Live video can be done across almost any social media platform, but be sure to apply the same rules that we discussed: keep it short and keep an eye on video quality. If all you want to do is show off people skating at your ice rink, then great—show it off!—but no one is going to want to watch people going in circles for 10 minutes. Due to quality issues that can arise with live video, especially when shooting inside, limit your live videos to under two minutes unless you really have something great to show off. There is also the notion of a produced, uncontrolled live video, where you are setting up a shot with lights and maybe some advanced audio. It will give you the feel of a live-but-high-quality video.

Controlled, live videos are more common, and they are typically much easier to execute. These are the videos you see when someone is sitting in front of a computer screen or holding a camera and talking. These are a fast, easy, and economical way to get your message out to your audience, and almost anyone can do it. Feel free to practice a few times or use cue cards to ensure that you're conveying the right message. Many companies miss the appeal of this method by having their CEO give out an important message to their fans. Sure, you can spend an hour or two creating an email, blasting it out with lots of lots of writing that will take your customers a long time to read, and copying and pasting your CEO's signature on the bottom. Or you can spend fifteen minutes preparing a two-minute live message given by the CEO, conveying not only the message but also hopefully some passion for the topic. Of course, doing both, as well as other follow-up forms of marketing, will always work best, but remember to consider video as a viable communication option.

CONTESTS AND QUESTIONS

Earlier in this chapter, I discussed why no one ever engages with your content, and I said that it was because you simply weren't asking them to. This is where you do exactly that because, after all, social media is supposed to be *social*. Asking questions on social media is a great way to get information from your audience, let them peer inside the 360-degree aspects of your brand, and have some fun. There are endless variations of questions you can ask, but typically, they come in two major categories: direct and indirect. A **direct question** is one that is right on point with your business. Examples would be:

1. Restaurant - What is your favorite burger topping?

2. Bank - What are you saving for?

3. Health Club - What's the best drink after a workout?

4. Mall - What is your favorite snack in our food court?

5. Real Estate Agent - How long have you lived in your current property?

All of these questions are centered around your business. Therefore, your audience should be familiar enough with the concept to want to answer these questions in one form or another. Don't feel like you have to try too hard to get your audience talking. Most of the time you should stick to the basics and provide a simple question—one that will have a simple answer.

Asking a question is also an excellent way to gauge how engaged your audience is with your social media platforms. For example, if you post a question and you get a ton of responses, then odds are that you've built a substantial audience. Good job! If you don't, check your marketing equation first (5 Steps) and ensure that you're actively marketing your question correctly, not just posting. If you still come up short with the number of answers you'd like, then you may have some work to do in building up a substantial core audience. *Refer back to Chapter 2, the part about the Facebook algorithm.*

Indirect questions are an entertaining and creative way to promote your brand. Think creatively, and ask something that has something to do with your brand but not necessarily your business. It could be almost anything. Here are a few examples from the same five categories above:

1. Restaurant - What food could you eat every single day and never get tired of?

2. Bank - Money is money, but _____ is priceless.

3. Health Club - My New Year's resolution is _____.

4. Mall - Share pictures and stories about meeting Santa at the mall!

5. Real Estate Agent - If I could live anywhere, it would be _____.

These questions are related to your industry but are more of a branding tool than anything else. They demonstrate the tone of your business to your users as well as what your brand is all about. In conjunction with other marketing content, asking questions can be a potent social media marketing tool. Of course, these questions are optional and will, therefore, take more effort than a simple click.

So, how do we get more people to interact with our questions? Incentivize them, of course. Contests are an incredible way to spread the word about your business, product, or event, and they can become a catalyst to letting your followers and fans do the work for you. How? Offer your users something in return for answering your question. You don't necessarily have to give something to everyone, so feel free to make it a raffle-type contest where everyone who enters has a chance to win XYZ.

Be sure to spell out *all* of the details in the text of your post, including when the contest begins and ends. Also, be sure to include what the user needs to do to enter as well as any restrictions. Retail companies have an advantage over everyone here as they can give away a candle, a hamburger, a book, etc. Other companies can also use contests–they just may have to get creative. Before you post a contest, be sure to check the rules of any social media site you post on, as breaking the rules can have some significant negative consequences.

Keep your contests simple! I can't stress this enough. Don't ask people to write a paragraph or post a video of themselves singing a song. Ask them who is their favorite Star Wars character, what is their favorite aspect of Fall, or who would they like to have dinner with. Keep this in line with graphics and pictures for your contest posts, and keep it simple. Keep your wording short and to the point, and remember: one idea at a time! This isn't to say that you can't ever run brash contests requiring people to go out of their way to enter; you just have to make the prize worth the effort. Make the juice worth the squeeze!

We'll focus more thoroughly on the idea of resource allocation for social media marketing campaigns later on. Still, please remember that people are being bombarded with literally hundreds, if not thousands, of messages every day. They'll only pay enough attention to do something if it is worth their time. Typically, the simpler the better. Remember the 80/20 rule? A good rule of thumb is that even if someone doesn't enter your contest, they should be able to glance at your posts for a moment and understand the overall concept. If you can pull that off, then you're really cooking with gas.

Don't forget to use the people who enter your contests as a way of getting others to do the same. In some cases you can ask them to tag a friend with the incentive that their friend will win too, or you could ask them to tag someone they would share the prize with. You'll stretch your budget much further if you can get your audience to share your posts as much as possible. Always check the rules of the platform you're on in regard to contests but remember: we pay for reach, but shares are just as good, and shares are *free*.

LOCATION-BASED CONTENT

The smartphone era ushered in the ability for marketers to have access to a user's location, pretty much anytime they want. As long as someone has their cell phone's location services turned on, social media sites can track their location. If you marry this technology with digital mapping (Google Maps, Apple Maps, etc.), you now have the makings of some exciting marketing opportunities, the major ones being geo-targeting, geo-fencing, and geo-filters.

Since we've already discussed the idea of **geo-targeting** earlier on in the chapter about finding the right audience, let's take a minute and build on it a bit. When targeting a user's location, there are ways to dive more deeply than just selecting the city or zip code that is most relevant. Most social media sites will give you the option to either find people who live, work, or will be traveling to and from a specific location. These are three distinct aspects that can be used for your marketing campaigns and traits that you might want to take into consideration. For example, if you are marketing a movie theater, then you are most likely going to want to geo-target users where they live because nobody really goes to the movies on their lunch break. If you are marketing a coffee shop, you want to target users who live and work in that location. Both people who live and work in a location can and will frequent a coffee shop. This distinction is just another layer of getting inside your audience's head and removing as much loss as possible by targeting more specifically.

Geo-fencing comes into play a little bit in social media, but it isn't a significant factor. Essentially, this is when you send users a message, but only if they enter a specific geographic location, like your store or shopping center. It is an opt-in service, so while you might show an ad as an impression to a user, the user still has to click on it in order to engage. This marketing tool is one that got (and still gets) business owners very excited because they often feel that they have something new that everyone will use. *Wow, now I can send a message to everyone who walks into my store!* They forget, however, that marketing hasn't changed, and your geo-fencing offer is only as good as someone being willing to engage with it. Using this tool is no different from any other marketing tool and must be vetted using the 5 Steps. If not, this tool can backfire in a big way, annoying your customers and coming off as spam.

The beauty of **geo-filtering** is that it's a value-added, user opt-in function. Essentially, a filter (or picture frame of sorts) that users can only get when they are in or around your specific business. The difference here is that you create a geo-filter that the user *wants* to use. There is a significant difference between geo-fencing—which is typically not a value-added function for the user, but more so for the business—and geo-filtering. For example, let's say you want to create a geo-filter for your minor league baseball team. For starters, you need to define your area. It's probably a good idea to put your filter (virtually) around your stadium property. It's also probably a good idea to make it fun and relatable to the baseball experience, and to put your logo on it somewhere. Why? Because if you have thousands of fans coming to your games throughout the season and taking pictures, you might as well have them taking pictures using your branded geo-filter (picture frame) and sending that out to their friends. If done correctly, you may have created a way for your fans to do the marketing work for you. Cool, huh?

An example of a geo-filter for a theme park. Users insert their own picture into the frame, and the words and logos appear on top. Users need to be in the physical location in order to access this geo-filter.

Geo-filters are also an excellent option for one-time uses like special events or holidays. Create a geo-filter for the Christmas Eve service at your church, the after-hours fundraiser for MS research, or even for your client's wedding or anniversary party. Remember, also, that just because the filter is there, it doesn't mean that somebody is necessarily going to use it. Go through the 5 Steps and market your filter as a call-to-action marketing campaign. Then, sit back and watch your customers promote your business to the world.

The last thing I want to mention is the idea of **location-based tagging,** sometimes referred to as a "check-in." It's where users use their location-based mobile device to virtually check-in at a business or virtually tag that business in a social media post. You can do this with your content as well. It is typically a fast and easy way for users to find out where other users are shopping, eating, etc. This is usually a significant part of the social media lifestyle and an effortless way for customers to give a virtual shout-out to your business. Remember that you still have to market this idea to make it work, and most likely you will have to ask users to do so to in order to take full advantage.

WHAT PLATFORMS SHOULD I BE POSTING ON?

Each social media marketing platform is different, and each has its own target audience as well. Discovering the demographic profile of each social media site is pretty easy to do: Google it. This information changes often and is readily available to anyone who wants it. Start by finding your audience. Then, find the social media platform that your audience fits or correlates with best. In many cases, using multiple social media sites at the same time is a good idea, as many will overlap with their demographics. Remember, though, that the major social media sites are vast—very vast—and in some cases, they encompass the majority of the number of people on the planet. Therefore, if you find that the social media sites you want to use only have a 25% usage rate among your core demographic, consider the size of the number of users on the entire platform. If that number is in the billions, then 25% of that is still a huge number of people. You don't take percentages to the bank: you take dollars. So always remember that all of the users you are going to interact with are real people, not just numbers.

So, what platforms should you be on? Well, not to frustrate you any more than I already have, but here's my answer: you should be on as many social media sites as you can commit to while running sound marketing campaigns consistently. So, if you only have the resources to be on one platform, then that's probably fine. Nothing is worse than doing a half-assed job on several sites: something that will most likely get you nowhere. Execution is *critical*, so don't get bogged down feeling like you need to be on every platform because you don't. Ideally, you should try to commit to being on a least a few of the significant sites, but don't bite off more than you can chew. If you do, you'll just get burnt out and probably quit the whole digital marketing thing altogether. Some of this is only human nature.

Take Bob, for example, who wants to write a blog (bear with me). The first blog that Bob writes is beautiful; it's six paragraphs with a nice picture. Good job, Bob! The next time Bob posts a blog is two weeks later, but this time it's three paragraphs with an ok picture. The next time Bob posts a blog is six weeks later, and its only one short paragraph with no picture. That is the last blog post that ever Bob writes. Why? He's just writing; he's not marketing. He does not have a specific reason to write a blog; he only heard it was a good idea. He also doesn't really have any idea how to use a blog to market his business and therefore, when he does and nobody reads it, it becomes a waste of time. This is an example of how many people approach social media marketing; they do it for a little bit with no strategic plan and then convince themselves that it doesn't work. A blog, as well as almost any social media site, can be (or become) a powerful marketing tool. As we discussed ad nauseam, all marketing campaigns have to be strategic and should fit somewhere within the 5 Step system. When they do, then your marketing campaigns have a purpose, and it's a lot harder to get burnt out when you have a plan and a purpose. Otherwise, you're just posting and essentially wasting your time.

8

Step #3 - Promote Your
Business as a Brand

Now that we've taken the time to define who our audience is and have come up with content that we think our audience will engage with, are we all set to post? No! There's still another important step that we need to consider before posting anything, and that's the idea of branding. We need to make sure that all of our posts represent our brand in a way that adds value to our business and makes a calculated, lasting impression in our audience's mind. To do this, though, we must first define what our brand is actually all about.

Branding can be an intimidating word for a lot of business owners. Many think about branding as a very long, drawn-out, and costly process. In some cases, it can be, and I always encourage businesses to define their "brand standards" including color schemes, fonts, voice, etc. However, that's not what we're talking about here. When I say "branding," I mean how you want your customers to perceive your business. You can figure this out in one quick exercise. Think about *the three things you want people to think about when they think about your business*. Some of these will be obvious: fresh, family-friendly, and elegant, etc. If you are a carpet cleaning company then yes, cleaning is probably one of your three branding elements, but be sure to also think about aspects that might not be so obvious.

Professionalism, dependability, hard work, and punctuality are all essential aspects that a lot of businesses want their customers to see in them as well. We do this exercise because we want to ensure that our audience sees our business the way *we want them to see it*, and sometimes those are two very different things. In your mind's eye you might regard your business as classy, modern, and trendy, and maybe it truly is. On the other hand, a quick look on your social media sites by an impartial user might give the impression of run-down, old fashioned, and bland. So while you think it's one thing, your customers (or potential customers) might be perceiving something far different. And remember, *perception is reality*.

When we post content on our social media pages, we are marketing our business to our core audience in the same way that we would with other forms of advertising. Therefore, we want to be sure that our content will create a lasting impression on our audience regarding what our business is all about. Our content, whether an impression or an engagement, needs to follow a set of standards in order to ensure that the message we are portraying regarding our business is clear and intentional. So, before we post anything on our social media pages, we need to filter our content through our *brand filter* to ensure that it is making the lasting impression that we desire. In order to do this, place any of your content up against your three major branding elements and be sure they are in line with one another. If not, change your content so that it falls within the branding guidelines. As you post content through your filter, you'll notice that certain elements will stand out more prominently than others. If one or two elements seem to be lacking, use this as an excuse to create content centered around those specific branding elements. In doing so, you'll find that your content will become more creative, and your audience will become more interested as a result.

THE ART OF POSITIONING

This idea of branding goes hand in hand with the concept of **positioning,** or distinct aspects of a brand that have become well-known in a particular audience's competitive set or mind. For example, when I ask, "What's the best place to buy a book online?" the majority of you think *Amazon*. Now, Amazon may be the best place to buy a book online, but it's not the only place. Nor did that idea just appear in your head overnight. The idea of "the best online book retailer" took time to develop. The idea grew slowly as you read about Amazon, saw advertisements about Amazon, heard other people talk about Amazon, and eventually tried Amazon for yourself. During the process, you were developing conscious and subconscious opinions about your understanding of buying books online and about a company called Amazon. You were, in fact, defining Amazon as a brand in your head.

Amazon, especially in the early days, worked hard to position themselves as the best online retailer for books and, of course, they eventually added other products. Positioning themselves as the best fit for their target audience required them to think far beyond having a lot of books and boxes in stock or coordinating shipping logistics. As a business, they had to consider ease of ordering, return policy, customer service, availability on different platforms, etc. As a brand, they had to find ways to market their business so that the perception of their brand would represent them as the best company from which order books online in the consumers' minds. Your business (probably in a smaller way) can and should do the same thing. Figure out who your audience is, and then figure out what you want your business to represent to that group of people. Lastly, do what it takes to position your brand in regard to that particular thing.

Notice how I didn't say that you *have to be the best* at what you do. Don't forget, we're talking about marketing here, and while *how* your company operates and takes care of its customers has a significant impact on your brand, it's not everything. In fact, how your business operates and interacts with its customers should be a function of marketing. Any action has to be taken within core branding standards, not the other way around. Here's the trick: you don't necessarily need to be the best if you have great marketing, but it does help.

For example, let's take my friend Carrie Luxem, who owns a company called Restaurant HR Group in Chicago. You can easily understand what she is positioning herself to be right away from the name of her business. Don't miss the message: Carrie is the best restaurant HR person around, no question about it. Still, she started marketing her business early on with a clear, concise message using social media marketing. She started using LinkedIn, and for about ten years she posted a short, non-produced video a few times a week. She spoke about restaurant human resources, leadership, and motivation: all significant aspects of her brand. Shortly after finding some success on LinkedIn, she expanded, taking her videos and messages to Facebook, Twitter, Instagram, and YouTube.

After a while, people from the restaurant industry in her part of the country (the Midwest) began to watch her videos fairly often, and then routinely. Before she knew it, she was running a restaurant human resources empire. Why? Because she's great at what she does (sure), but more importantly, when anyone in the restaurant industry in the Midwest thought about restaurant human resources, they thought of Carrie. So, while there may be another restaurant HR company somewhere in the Midwest that has a competitive advantage over the way Carrie does things (I doubt it), it doesn't matter very much. Why? Because Carrie has positioned herself as the expert within a targeted audience, and that is some good marketing. What Amazon and Carrie both did well was the gold standard of marketing and business: they created a great product and marketed it to the right people with the right content, all rolled up in a solid branding position and backed by the right amount of resources. They backed up the promise of their marketing by doing as good of a job as they had advertised. So, if you can pull that off, then you're going to be just fine!

THE IMPORTANCE OF USING VARIOUS FORMS OF CONTENT

As you work to communicate your brand through creative content, you need to remember that your brand is a living, breathing organism. Whether you're marketing something tangible (offers, new products, events) or intangible (excellent service, neighborhood vibe, honesty), you need to use various forms of content. Some content will work better than others in terms of communicating multiple aspects of your brand. This is where the idea of **varied content** comes into play: using a myriad of different kinds of content for marketing purposes.

Some of this is obvious. If you add a new pizza topping to your menu, hen you post a beautiful picture of your new pizza topping and let your audience know that it's new and is now for sale. But what if your new pizza topping is gluten-free and has been added to grow your ever-popular gluten-free menu? Your approach to this might be different. Aside from just posting about your new topping, you might explain "why" and tell the story behind the decision. Then, you would find creative ways to do so. Don't just post! Don't post that one picture you have of the pizza topping over and over again, because nobody is going to pay attention to that! Use your marketing brain and come up with some great content that communicates your brand, and use things that will make your business stand out. Below is an expanded example:

Joe's Pizza Restaurant

New Gluten-Free Pizza Toppings Campaign

Social Media Marketing Ideas

Branding Standards for Joe's Pizza

1. Fresh

2. Family

3. Fun

Here is what the first week of this promotion might look like on social media:

Day #1 - A high-quality picture of the new pizza topping and an explanation of how it is sourced locally and prepared daily with a short explanation of what it is. (Fresh)

Day #2 - A short, low-quality, unproduced video of one of your customers talking about how they just tried the new pizza topping and they love it because their son has celiac disease. As a mom, she really appreciates all of the great, gluten-free options. (Fresh, Family)

Day #3 - A promotion for your weekly, family pizza game night. (Fresh, Family, Fun)

Day #4 - An article about a local, family-friendly charity event going on in your community. (Family)

Day #5 - A high-quality, produced video about your gluten-free pizza menu, highlighting the new menu item and the fact that you are a family-owned business with lots of happy employees. Show customers in the b-roll having a great time. (Fresh, Family, Fun)

Day #6 - A low-quality picture of your fruit and vegetable delivery guy bringing in a daily shipment of produce. (Fresh)

Day #7 - A funny comic strip about pizza. (Fun)

Notice how, during this week of social media marketing, the restaurant represented their brand very well. Notice also how many different forms of content they posted, leveraging themself to become a pretty impressive social media page for their customers to want to go and check out from time to time. During the first week, they only posted three times about the gluten-free menu items. Why? Because Joe's is not a gluten-free restaurant or business, and gluten-free is not one of their core brand standards. It is, in fact, an essential aspect of the restaurant, but Joe's Pizza does not (in this case) want to be thought of as gluten free in their customers' minds more than fresh, family, and fun. Joe's core business, and therefore brand, is centered on families coming in for a good time to have some freshly prepared pizza. So, even though they want to push their gluten-free menu right now, it is imperative that they go back to their brand standards to ensure that they communicate a sound message.

Furthermore, if Joe's Pizza wants to become known primarily for gluten-free pizza, then they can change or add this to their brand standards. Remember, the exercise of coming up with the three aspects of your brand is to be used as a tool, not a rule. It's your business, so do what you want! Just remember that the type of content that you post is, and will become, a direct reflection of your brand. Just for fun, here's what *not* to do:

Joe's Pizza Restaurant

New Gluten-Free Pizza Toppings Campaign

Social Media Marketing Ideas

Branding Standards for Joe's Pizza

1.   Fresh

2. Family

3. Fun

Here is what the first week of this promotion might look like on social media:

Day #1 - A low-quality picture of the new pizza topping with two paragraphs of wording explaining how you offer gluten-free pizzas as part of your catering packages. (None)

Day #2 - A graphic designed to be a flyer with a ton of text on it, promoting your Tuesday drink specials. (None)

Day #3 - An "adult-themed" Kermit the Frog meme about pizza. (Actually clashes with your family brand standard)

Day #4 - A graphic designed to be a flyer, with a ton of text, promoting your Thursday drink specials. (None)

Day #5 - The same low-quality picture and post from Day #1... (None)

Day #6 - The same low-quality picture and post from Day #1 and Day #5... (None)

Day #7 - Someone takes a picture with their phone of your printed gluten-free menu and posts it. (None)

Hopefully, you are starting to see how the branding element of your social media content is the driving factor behind everything you do. It all comes down to the 30,000-foot view of what you want a particular group of people to think about when they think about your business. Too often, businesses post far too many specials, promotions, and coupons on their pages and then wonder why this doesn't produce results. The answer is simple: you are probably not a business that offers discounts and promotions as a product. People then do not pay much attention to your posts, or they even might go as far as unfollowing you if they are not anticipating or wanting this kind of content from you. They followed your business because they *like* your business, your products, your service, and your people, etc. So give them that. Build the brand on social media the same way you would if someone walked into your business for the first time. Would offering your products at a discount be the first thing that you say to them? Probably not. The first thing that you would probably do is talk about how amazing your products are, how excellent your service is, or how you can help them get what they need or want. For some reason, when it comes to social media, some businesses seem to forget this and focus on looking desperate. Don't do it!

The amazing thing here is that when you build your audience the right way, and with the right content, you now have an excellent platform of interested users who will hear you when you have something to say. When you want to promote a new special or even a discount on your social media pages, your followers will be so excited that you are giving them something that they will be all over your content. Remember, the best and the most impactful social media pages drive engagement from their audience and promote a business's brand.

To bring this all together, let's say that your business *is* about offering discounts, promotions, and coupons. Maybe you run a service that promotes specials of companies in a particular local area. Then, offering discounts and promotions *is your product*. So post away. Even so, these businesses would also have other aspects that would need to be brought forward and communicated via positioning and using varied content. Regardless of the product, the overall branding message should be taken into consideration for any marketing strategy.

The last point to keep in mind is the 80/20 rule that we talked about earlier: 80% of people will not read anything on your page. Therefore, your goal should be that if someone scans one of your social media pages and doesn't read one word, they should still have a clear picture of what your brand is all about. It's a great exercise to try for yourself. Write down your three branding elements: the three things you want people to think about when they think about your business. Then, scan your own social media pages without reading anything and see for yourself how well your branding elements are being communicated. If it's not where you want it to be, go back, use the 5 Steps, and fix it.

9

Step #4 - Use Ample Resources

If there is one crucial tool that anyone can use to grow their social media pages, it's money: or should I say, money backed by strategy. We've already defined the idea of finding the right audience, creating the right content for that audience, and promoting your business as a brand, so now it's time to figure out how many people in that audience we can actually reach. The first step, of course, is to find out the total number of people in our audience and then to do some simple math.

When researching your audience on any social media platform, you need to find the total number of users who fit into that category and who could potentially see your content. Interests and geography will be the major players here, so use these as determining factors to adjust and fine-tune the size of the potential audience you want to reach. At this time, we need to take into consideration our **budget**, or the amount of money we are able to spend on our social media campaigns. It is going to be a significant factor in determining how many people we potentially reach within our target audience. When thinking about budgets, you should try to do so on more of a macro scale than a micro one. If you can, work out a budget for as long of a time as possible—say, a month, a quarter, or a year—as opposed to just one week or one day. This is because we are trying to run sound marketing campaigns that make an impact over time. Consistency is vital. Also, because our social media campaigns may not work the way we want them to the first time around, we need to have enough money to be able to create efficiency and to learn from our mistakes and failures. This also helps because we will most likely have to show our content to the people in our audience multiple times in order to get them to do what we want them to. Typically, the more time we have, the better. Sure, there will be times when you might need to push hard on a specific, short-term campaign, but try to figure out a budget that you can use consistently, however that might make sense for you and your business.

As I've stated ad nauseam, social media marketing is no different from any other kind of marketing and works well when it is *consistent*. If you don't believe me, consider several of the world's most popular brands like Coca-Cola, Harley Davidson, State Farm, or Disney. These brands, on an enormous scale, have consistently remained popular by promoting the same brand for decades. You can counter this with any one-hit-wonder or 15-minutes-of-fame product or business that just couldn't cut it. Did they fail because they didn't have a superior product? Maybe, but good companies find ways to adapt to market conditions and effectively and consistently communicate a clear marketing message. What you need to do is decide if you are in this for the short term or the long haul. Knowing this will help you determine where your budget should be.

CALCULATING A CPM (COST PER 1000 IMPRESSIONS)

Determining the CPM for your social media campaign can be done in one of two ways: either you calculate an estimation while you're creating your ad, or you run some ads first and let the results uncover your CPM. Of course, opting to do both is the best and most beneficial way. Remember, a CPM is the measurement of the cost per 1,000 impressions, or how much it costs to show your ad to 1,000 people at a time. During the audience-defining aspect of building an ad on almost any social media platform, you will most likely be given a target audience range as well as an estimated cost variance. These estimations can be vast: up to thousands of users and hundreds of dollars. However, if you play around and do some quick math, you should get a ballpark number of what your CPM might be. To do this, divide the total estimated audience reach by one thousand, then divide the total estimated spending by the CPM multiplier and you'll have your estimated CPM. Here is what that looks like:

Estimated Audience Size: 45,000

Estimated Daily Cost: $20 to reach an estimated 2,500 people

2,500 / 1,000 (M) = 2.5 CPM multiplier

$20 / 2.5 = 8

CPM = $8

Once we've done this and once we've run our ads, then we want to go back and run the same equations with the actual numbers. This way, you know exactly what your CPM was for your campaign and you can compare that to what you've estimated. It goes back to the scientific method idea that we discussed earlier. It gives you a good idea of where you were in regard to your pre-campaign estimated CPM hypothesis and where you're at based on your actual spending.

You can also run a similar equation in order to figure out how many people you can reach if you have a **set budget** or a specific amount of money that you have to spend. You need three pieces of information to do this: the number of people in your target audience, the amount of money you have to spend, and the CPM is for your specific audience. For example, if my target audience is 100,000 people and the CMP of that audience is

$10, but I only have $100 to spend, then I can reach 10,000 people for my $100, or 10% of the audience I am targeting. Here's what that looks like:

100,000 people in the target audience

$10 CPM

$100 budget

$100 budget / $10 CPM = 10

10 x 1,000 (M) = 10,000 people

10,000 people / 100,000 target audience = 10% of target audience

Analyzing the numbers like this take the guesswork out of coming up with the right budget for your social media campaigns. In this case, we based our reach on the budget within a defined target audience. One of the things we need to keep a close eye on is the number of people in our total target that we can reach. If you feel (in this case) that 10% of your entire audience is too low, and you have set a budget of only $100, then the only choice you have is to reduce the total audience to a more efficient, manageable number.

You may want to reduce the geographic range, or you may want to get more specific with your interests and behavioral targeting. What you are doing here is fine-tuning your target audience due to lack of, or at least restricted, resources. Doing so will help your content and brand to not "get lost" by being shown to lots of people using relatively general demographics. Unless you always have an abundant budget, you will most likely be running campaigns to a smaller, more targeted audience. The other benefit of doing this is to capitalize on what makes your audience "special or different." For example, let's say you decided to whittle down a marketing campaign's audience from reaching the entire Midwest (2 million people) to just Wisconsin (450,000 people). You may be reaching fewer people, but you can use the fact that all the users you are reaching live in Wisconsin. So use content elements that appeal to people in Wisconsin.

The less money you have to spend, the smaller your audience is typically going to be. Let's say that you are selling concert tickets for a famous band near a major city and you have a limited budget. Your initial findings on the fans of your group on a specific platform are over one million people in the state in which you are promoting. Your advertising dollars, however, are limited, so you might only be able to reach a fraction of the total audience size. Therefore, you might need to reduce the size of your audience by putting a 30-mile radius around the concert venue, which may reduce your total audience size from, let's say, 1,000,000 to 150,000, which will allow you to now reach 15% of the entire audience: a much more manageable number. You are also creating better efficiency with your marketing dollars by using them to target the people who you feel will be both interested and also have the shortest traveling distance.

Another way to approach this is to allow the audience to determine the size of their budget. First, define the target audience and figure out the CPM, *then* figure out what percentage of the target audience you want to reach consistently. With that information in hand, run your equation to determine how much money you need to reach the right amount of people in your audience. Doing it this way takes *all* the guesswork out of the equation completely, and allows you to have complete control over how many people you are reaching. Let's say you have an audience of 100,000 people and your goal is reach 20% of that audience every month. How much money you should budget for? Below is an example of what this equation would look like:

100,000 people in the target audience

$10 CPM

The goal is to reach 20% of people in the target audience every month

20% of 100,000 people is 20,000 people

20,000 people / $10 CPM = $200

The budget recommendation is $200 per month

This approach also allows you to potentially reach all of the people in your target audience over time. If you reach 20% of the target audience every month and run your campaign for five months, then, by the end of the fifth month, you should have reached everyone with at least one impression (100%). Remember, though, that these numbers are theoretical, and you will often reach users multiple times: something referred to as the **frequency of impressions,** or how many times each user sees your content and is counted as an impression. It basically means that if I am in your audience, you could reach me ten times over the course of five months with ten different impressions. So, while I personally received ten impressions, you didn't reach ten different people with those ten impressions, you only reached one.

This plays into what I am going to refer to as the **20/20 rule**, meaning that you should try to reach at least 20% of your target audience consistently and then get 20% of those people to engage with your content regularly. Remember, the goal of your social media campaigns is to achieve engagement, not just to reach. So, if we're able to reach 20% of our audience during a set period, and then get another 20% to engage with our content, we are getting, in our running example, 4,000 engagements from our target audience every time we spend $200.

Let's look at how to calculate this using a previous example from the chapter. In this case, we are going to set our period for one month. So, if our goal is to reach 20% of our total audience every month, how much money do we need to spend every month in order to achieve this? Knowing that our CPM is $8, and our entire audience is 45,000, we start by calculating 20% of 45,000, which is 9,000 people. Then, we divide the 9,000 by 1,000, which is 9. We multiply that by our $8, which is $72. So, if we spend $72 on our ads every month, we will reach 20% of our total audience during that period. Here's what that looks like below:

45,000 in target audience * .20 (or 20%) = 9,000

9,000 / 1,000 (M) = 9

9 * $8 (CPM) = $72

While some might balk and say this is far too low, if you can achieve the 20/20 rule in your social media marketing, then your campaigns will be successful more often than not. Moreover, it is a way to gauge the success of your campaigns, and this is light years away from just waking up and posting every day. Sure, you might be able to do better—much better!—but now you have a way to measure it. The point in all of this is to take the guesswork out of your budgets by using strategic applications. Therefore, when you are trying to figure out how much money to spend on a particular campaign, don't guess! Run the 5 Steps. Find your target audience and define the total number of people and CPM, figure out what kinds of content you need to create to properly promote your campaign to this audience, and ensure that you are using your brand filter.

OTHER THINGS TO BUDGET FOR

Content creation, however, is not always free and not always cheap. Time and talent need to be taken into consideration in regard to your budget as well, and you need to figure out what expenses you'll incur while producing the content for your campaigns. If you have a graphic designer on staff then great, but some of you might need to hire one. If you can create the graphics yourself, that's fine too. If you need to produce videos, develop geo-filters, or have high-quality pictures taken, you'll need to figure out the cost of making these happen as well. Keep in mind that while, in a perfect world, it's great to let your campaigns determine the appropriate budgets, in reality, this is not always possible. Therefore, in regard to your budgets, always take the time to do the research and calculate how much you think it is going to cost to successfully run a particular campaign. Next, compare this to your actual budget and manage it accordingly. So, if your campaign calls for high-quality video, but you can't afford it, don't substitute low-quality video and just "get it done." Get creative and use a different form of content that is both affordable and high-quality. Below are the steps you should take when determining how much money you'll need for your campaign:

1. Figure out the total number of people in your target audience, along with the CPM.

2. Figure out how much money will be required to reach 20% of your audience consistently, at a minimum. (the 20/20 rule)

3. Determine the appropriate kinds of content needed for each campaign, and the cost of producing each piece. (graphics, videos, etc.)

4. Add #2 and #3 together.

5. Calculate your actual budget for your campaign and compare this to #4.

6. Adjust the audience size and content production as needed to fit the budget, while still achieving the 20/20 rule.

7. Wash, rinse, and repeat.

TIME IS MONEY

Remember, too, that you are not always necessarily running social media marketing campaigns in isolated situations. As previously discussed, we are trying to achieve branding by producing many call-to-action steps over time. In most cases, this will force you to distribute your budgets between various events, offers, calls-to-action, and branding pieces, etc. A classic example of this is the marketing manager of a coffee shop that has live music. This manager has a budget for the month and needs to market coffee drinks, pre-packaged retail coffee, food, the dining room, live music events, and—of course—the brand. This manager needs to determine how to allocate the budget in order to achieve optimal call-to-action on the events and products. They also need to achieve ample brand communication by promoting several things at once. This can be a difficult task which most likely requires a solid foundational understanding of each platform that is going to be used as well as a keen understanding of timing.

Time is, of course, a resource, and perhaps the most valuable and scarce resource that we have. When you have a lot of aspects of your business to promote, approach them from the standpoint of inventory. Since you have already determined the scope of each aspect, and you have determined an effective cadence for your posts, you now have to play the timing game. Pace out your posts and events using the varied content rule. Be mindful about how much information users on your pages can handle at any given time. If you are promoting a significant event, consider any marketing farther than three weeks out as a tease. Then, gradually increase the frequency of your posting and your resource allocation as you lead up to the day of the event. Don't waste too much time early on with a call-to-action campaign. Use your resources to build anticipation with your call-to-action and message.

Do not *ever* think that you can just post the day before an event for the first time and achieve successful results. Stranger things have happened, but getting ahead of our posts, and having a calendar or strategy in place will not only be beneficial for your budget, it will also help to keep the pacing of your content on track. Sometimes, times get tough and we feel the need to push harder than we'd like, but don't throw away your long-term brand standards for short-term gains. Stay true to your business and post in accordance with how you want your customer base to interpret your brand.

Remember when you put money behind a post by boosting or advertising, it will not be shown for only one day, but for many days. You can also consider the fact that some of the ads you run will not show up on your social media pages at all. These are referred to as **dark ads** or ads that reach the target audience, but do not show up on the timeline of a business. You use these when you have a big idea or an ongoing event that needs to be promoted, and you don't necessarily want to jumble up your page with the same content all the time. These types of ads are typically created on an ad platform separate from your business timeline. They typically achieve the same results as boosted posts, but they usually give the marketer more advanced tools to use. You're going to want to use both of these types of ads.

Use organic content to paint a picture of your brand within the chosen social media platform, all the while pacing out the dollars within your budget. What I mean is that you should never let one idea or event overrun your brand on your social media pages. Let's say that your boutique is running a big holiday sale; this is something that you may want to run for a few weeks leading up to Christmas. The goal would be to promote the holiday sale heavily while still maintaining the cadence and branding of the page. Therefore, running one or two dark ads that are continually pushing out impressions to your target audience might make sense, all while posting about the holiday sale a few times a week on the business page. I want to be clear; you can't push any idea about something you need to get done too hard. If you need to run ten different ads for your big upcoming event, then go for it. You simply need to achieve balance in your posting and your branding. A good marketing manager can consistently promote a business's brand on social media, all the while delivering strong engagement and an even stronger call-to-action participation.

YOU HAVE TO SPEND MONEY TO MAKE MONEY

It is also important to note that in most cases, no matter how good your content is, if you don't have enough of a budget to reach your audience, you are just wasting your time. I have run into many business owners over the years who have incredible content on their social media pages, but very little (or in some cases zero) engagement or reach on any of their content. The most common example is a business that invests in having a lot of videos or professional pictures. These videos and photos look great on their video channel or in social media galleries. (Seriously, they do!) Still, without the right marketing strategy and budget, that great content sadly sits there and collects dust. I can't tell you how many YouTube channels I've seen with hundreds of great videos that have been there for years, all with less than fifty views per video. This, of course, is fine if you are using it as something of a landing page, for some reason. But why would you want to invest all of those resources on something that barely impacts anyone? So remember: no matter the marketing platform—be it your social media, your website, or your video channel—you need to have a strategic plan and ample resources in order to ensure that your content is going to be seen. Usually, this will justify the cost of creating the content in the first place.

Most of you will no doubt be faced with less-than-ideal budgets, and with inferior content compared to what you would, ideally, imagine. Don't let this get in the way of your progress. In fact, use it as a way to be more creative and unique. Social media is a playground for good marketing, and if something doesn't work, oh well, move on and try something else! If all you have is a low-quality video and simple graphics, then find ways to exploit aspects of your business where low-quality video and simple graphics are an *asset*. As the old cliché goes, the only time you can break the rules is when you know what the rules are. So do the research and do your homework on what you need to do to be successful. Then, take what you've got, break the rules, and run some killer marketing campaigns.

10

Step #5 - Analyze the Results

The one step that business owners and marketers miss more often than any other is *analyzing the results*. I believe that this is done, not intentionally, but because of the fast-paced world of digital marketing (and marketing in general). Typically, when something either works well or doesn't work at all, we're quick to move onto the next project. Regardless of the demands of our jobs, analyzing the results is a crucial step that separates good marketers from great ones. When it comes to your campaigns, it is essential to understand the difference between statistics and revenue. **Statistics** are the numbers that you use to analyze the validity of your social media campaigns. **Revenue** is money that you put in the bank. Both are important, and in this chapter we're going to deal primarily with statistics as a means of analyzing the success of our social media campaigns. I realize that, when dealing with statistics, we are not dealing with dollars and cents. Rather, we are determining whether or not the money we spent on our campaigns was worth it as compared to the revenue we earned in return.

Marketing is an essential part of any business's success. There are an infinite number of marketing options ranging from media buys, to community management, to public relations, to traditional marketing, etc., all of which have their own particular form of analytical resources. Digital marketing and social media are no different, but these platforms have an overabundance of analytics as compared to almost any of their competitors.

Of course, the overarching metric to use when analyzing a digital marketing campaign (or any kind, for that matter) is revenue or **ROI** (return on investment). Essentially, this is a comparison between the amount of money you spend on something versus the amount of money you earned from it. While many business owners will argue ROI is the *only* way to measure the success of a marketing campaign, I feel that they are missing a deeper understanding of the discipline. Over the years, I have spoken to many business owners, often restaurant owners. They'll tell you the same story every time:

"All I want you to do is fill up my restaurant."

"I don't care how much it costs, as long as it fills up my restaurant."

"All you marketing guys are the same. None of you can ever fill up my restaurant."

Anytime I'm faced with these or similar questions, I always offer the same response. I tell the restaurant owner, "That's not actually what you really want me to do." They respond, "*Of course* it is!" Then, I tell them that I'll go ahead and fill up their restaurant next Thursday by putting their business on Groupon at 75% off, and they'll receive twenty-five cents on the dollar. It's a sure-fire way to fill up the restaurant, no problem. Once they digest this information and inform me (I was right) that this is *not* what they want me to do, we start talking about filling up (or bringing in) the right customers, at the right price, and over the right amount of time. Eventually, we get into a conversation about branding and building a customer base. Now we're on our way to a sound marketing conversation and a sound marketing partnership.

The point is that you can't measure the success of a marketing campaign by one simple metric; you need *many*. If the restaurant owner based the success of a marketing campaign solely on the amount of revenue it produced and ultimately threw away sound business practices and branding, then he or she might think that the campaign was a success when it wasn't. So, in the same way that you would use metrics in order to evaluate your personal or business finances properly, you need to use several metrics to tell the entire story of your marketing campaign. In the case of the restaurant owners and Groupon, if they increased revenue by 50% by discounting products by 75% then they would have a negative ROI. Sure, you increased revenue (or filled up your restaurant), but you didn't achieve a positive financial return. By looking at only one metric you are missing a very important aspect of the overall marketing and business strategy. As previously stated, you can use all kinds of analytics for social media evaluation. Still, we are going to focus on three major aspects: **reach, engagement, and growth.**

THREE MAJOR ANALYTICAL METRICS

We've already discussed **reach** throughout this book, primarily in the previous chapter about using ample resources. Reach, of course, is the number of people we could possibly, or actually will, reach with our social media campaigns. It is the number of impressions: the number of people who saw our content. When we budget, we do so based on reach because this is the only aspect that we can control with our advertising dollars. The concept is relatively straightforward: if the current market states that it costs me X amount of dollars to reach Y amount of people, then that's the way it is. Knowing the extent of your reach will help you to understand how many of those people you are able to penetrate with your advertising dollars: the actual cost of your CPM.

Engagement is defined as the number of interactions with your content. This is not something that you can control with your budget because you can't directly *buy* engagements. Engagement is something you *earn* by first, creating the right content and then, getting your target audience to interact with it. Engagement is a very valuable metric when evaluating the success of your social media marketing campaigns. No matter how you slice it, a lack of engagement will almost always result in unsuccessful digital marketing campaigns.

Growth is the metric used to track how many new followers (or fans) you earn as a result of engagement with your social media marketing campaigns. For example, let's say I run a marketing campaign for $20 to reach 5,000 people. During my campaign, 1,000 of those people engage with my content and, as a result, 50 new people follow my page. Having 50 new followers will now increase my organic reach, resulting in me needing less money to reach my targeted number of people on a regular basis.

Growth works hand in hand with engagement to increase the likelihood that more people will see my posts organically. Growth is also an excellent way of measuring whether or not I'm reaching the *right people*. If I am reaching the right people with my content and they are interacting with it, then the number of users who choose to follow my page as a result will be a reliable indicator that those people are interested in seeing more of my content. Basically, this means that if I create the right content and *pay* to show it to the right audience, that audience should choose to follow my content *organically*. For example, I might be able to gain a ton of engagement to my social media pages by paying to advertise a hilarious picture that has nothing to do with my business. While this engagement is great, if none of the engaged audience is interested enough in my business to follow my page organically, then I am probably reaching the wrong audience. I am also probably wasting my money and my time. Remember, engagement is not the goal: engagement from the right audience, all the while communicating your brand, *is*.

This idea goes hand in hand with the importance of accurate evaluation of which people are following your social media pages. You have probably seen ads for services that promise to increase your number of social media followers for a fee: something like, "I can get you 10,000 Instagram followers by Friday for $34.95." While most of these services can and will do just that, consider whether or not this is truly the best approach. If you are an ice cream shop in St. Louis, what is the value of having people who live in Alaska, Germany, and Paris following your page? Not much. The idea of growing your pages the right way ensures that you have the *right* people following your pages. When done correctly, social media becomes a positive cycle: the more content you put out, the more frequently your target audience engages, the more followers your page earns, and so on and so on. You spend money on ads (or boosts) to reach your target audience, then get them to engage with your content and choose to follow your pages.

The success of a marketing campaign can be evaluated quite simply by accessing the analytical or insightful tools of almost any social media platform and looking at the demographic breakdown of your followers. This information is free and typically very easy to gather. Virtually every social media platform will provide the manager or admin of a page with the location, age, and gender of their core audience. All you have to do is evaluate this data based on who you have defined as your target audience and make sure you are reaching the right people with your hard-earned marketing dollars.

Using the 5 Steps (or any marketing strategy for that matter), we now can identify and correct any issues with our marketing campaigns as they arise. First, however, we need to know what we're looking for. Applying the analytical metrics of reach, engagement, and growth, we create a structure within which to drive the success of our campaigns and make adjustments in real time. We'll know whether or not our campaigns are working for us, and we'll be able to evaluate how well we have executed the marketing equation. For example, let's look at the analysis of two separate social media marketing campaigns on Facebook:

Account Name	Dates	Spend	FB Reach	FB Engagement	FB Followers	(Growth) New FB Followers
Joe's Pizza	1/1 - 1/7	$100	10,123	2,171	5,094	16
Account Name	Dates	Spend	FB Reach	FB Engagement	FB Followers	(Growth) New FB Followers
Brad's Pizza	1/1 - 1/7	$100	10,291	391	15,611	1

Knowing what you know now about social media marketing, you should be able to identify several key differences between these two accounts rather quickly. For the sake of argument, let's assume that both pizza restaurants are pretty much the same and that they both reside in similar communities. The first thing you should notice is that both pages spent the same amount of money and reached about the same amount of people (10,123 vs 10,291). As far as engagement scores go, Joe's did much better at 21% (2,171 / 10,123) than Brad's at 2.9% (391 / 10,291). Notice, too, that Joe's picked up sixteen new followers as opposed to Brad's one new follower. If we apply the 20/20 rule, then Joe's is doing well by achieving over a 20% engagement score to his target audience, while Brad's is pretty far behind. Without actually looking at the accounts, you should be able to conclude that the marketing team behind Joe's is doing well, while those executing Brad's marketing are not. Of course, Brad's team could just be having a bad week, but based solely on the numbers, these results are less than ideal. On that topic, it is crucial to understand the idea of **blips and trends. Blips** are periods of time where your marketing performs well outside what you typically expect from your campaign, but the event is short-lived and quickly bounces back to normal. **Trends** are extended periods of time where less-than-ideal, or overachieving numbers begin to become the norm. So, while you are most likely not going to hit your numbers out of the park every week, you want to be sure that you are aware enough of your statistical expectations to ensure that any negative blips don't become trends.

Blips and trends can also be positive, as sometimes you might see a huge spike in engagement or followers for one reason or another. Either way, the trick is to always investigate *why* this happened. If you know the problem, or you know what's working well, you can then make adjustments. In doing so, you can either steer your campaigns back on track or exploit a certain positive aspect and work it into your ongoing campaign strategy. Without tracking your numbers, though, these variances are very hard to see.

It is also interesting that Joe's numbers for the week, while satisfactory, weren't exactly fantastic. If, however, he continued to consistently earn those numbers over a long period of time, he could have something special. Any good marketer should work hard to consistently produce above-average results which, over time, turn into an amazing body of work. You'll have some great weeks, and you'll have some bad ones. Still, if you can consistently achieve the 20/20 rule – *reach 20% of your target audience and get 20% of those people to engage with your content* - all the while producing ample page growth within your target audience, then your social media marketing campaigns are going to be a success, no question about it. Even when the business owner in you says, "But what kind of an ROI is this?" remember that digital and social media are no different from any other form of marketing. So, whether you buy a billboard, a radio spot, or put an ad in a magazine, the same rules apply. You need to reach the right people with the right branded content, using ample resources, and then analyze your campaigns using reach, engagement, and growth. If you achieve the 20/20 rule, your business is naturally going to be positively impacted - as you communicated your marketing message properly to people you have identified as your core audience. No other answer makes logical sense.

As previously stated, another significant benefit of analyzing campaigns in this way is that we now know *how* to adjust our campaigns in real-time. More importantly, though, we know *when* to adjust our campaigns. Below is another example of social media data pulled after the first week of a four-week campaign on Instagram. What do you think?

Account Name	Dates	Spend	IN Reach	IN Engagement	IN Followers	IN New Followers
AJ's Flowers	9/1 - 9/7	$250	32,391	109	151	0

In this case, AJ's is reaching a ton of people (over 32,000), but hardly anybody is interacting with their posts (low engagement 109/32,391 = 3.3%), and therefore no new people are following their page (0 new followers). My guess is that the audience they are reaching and the content they are putting out both need to be adjusted. This is good news, though, because AJ's can make adjustments to their four-week marketing campaign after just one week by pausing and fixing the content and execution. Let's assume that they did so and then let's look at the numbers for the second week.

Account Name	Dates	Spend	IN Reach	IN Engagement	IN Followers	IN New Followers
AJ's Flowers	9/8 - 9/14	$250	24,337	3,951	165	14

Notice how AJ's campaigns reached far fewer people for the same amount of money (about 24,000 as opposed to 32,000), but their numbers demonstrate considerable improvement in engagement (3,951/24,337 = 16.2%) as well as a few new followers (14). The adjustments made to this campaign were the right adjustments, and AJ's is now starting to reach the right people with the right content; and it's starting to work. AJ's can use this progress and build on their success, continuing to fine-tune their campaigns until they figure out the exact right audience, right content, etc. for this particular campaign (maybe even to achieve the 20/20 rule!). In doing so, AJ's uses their marketing dollars efficiently and makes a significant impact in the world of their target audience. Besides reach, engagement, and growth, however, there are several other metrics that you should be aware of in the world of digital marketing. I'd like to walk you through a few of them.

OTHER IMPORTANT METRICS

CPC, or cost per click, is the amount of money you pay for a user to click on your content. This number becomes very important if you are running a campaign where your call-to-action involves the user clicking the post in order to do what you want them to do. For example, you'll want to know what the cost per click is if you are running a contest that requires users to enter by visiting a landing page. As with other metrics, if you are committed to your marketing for the long haul, and you organize and keep track of your results, you'll be able to determine an ample CPC for your campaigns. When doing so, you'll now know if you're paying too much or too little for clicks along the way, and you'll be able to use that information to adjust and fine-tune your campaigns moving forward. CPC analysis is typically still built upon the purchase of impressions to your target audience. To calculate this number, you can divide the number of clicks by the amount of money you spent. There is, however, another way.

PPC, or pay per click, is similar to CPC except when running PPC ads you only pay when someone clicks on your ad. For example, if you showed your ad to 10,000 people and nobody clicked on it, you would owe $0. PPC is typically how marketers buy Google Ads. Even though you are only paying when someone clicks, however, the same rules of marketing apply. To make your PPC campaigns valuable, you'll still need to determine the size of your target audience, figure out the right content to show to them, and then figure out what an appropriate PPC is for your business. Determining your PPC has more to do with your business model than anything else. If you are a roofing company whose average job costs

$10,000, then a $50-$100 PPC might make sense. This is different from a shoe store whose average sale ranges from $75-$100.

Conversions are another interesting concept to be aware of, but be cautious with this one. The word conversion can mean almost anything, and is typically a user-defined evaluation, meaning that *you* determine what, exactly, a conversion is, not the platform. Businesses can define conversions several ways ranging from a click, to a response, to a sale, to a video view. Conversions are built into almost all social media and digital marketing platforms, but you need to be sure that you understand how these are being captured. One of the best ways to use conversions as a robust evaluating tool is to determine whether or not a customer made a purchase. It's done by putting a pixel (or something similar) on your website which is connected to your digital marketing platform (Facebook, for example). You set the digital platform to mark a conversion when the user hits a specific page or button on your website. Many companies configure their pixels to flag the "thank you for your order page," so the system knows that the customer did, indeed, make a purchase.

For example, Jeff sells popcorn online and is running digital marketing campaigns. He configures a pixel on his website to work with Facebook using the following rules: run ads to all people on my target audience list, but remove them if the user reaches the "thank you for your ordering page." Jeff then uses a pixel to place all users who ordered his products online onto a new list encouraging them to subscribe to his email list. The pixel on his campaign will now consider a conversion to be a user who reaches the "thank you for subscribing" page. This type of conversion tracking works well if you sell products online, and it is the most accurate way to calculate an ROI on your digital marketing campaigns. Even if you do this, of course, tracking and evaluating your campaigns using reach, engagement, and growth still has merit and will paint an even more accurate picture about how well your marketing campaigns are performing. Feel free to get creative with your conversions and configure this system in a way that makes sense for your business.

Leads are a way of directly collecting users' information that request more details about a particular product or service. Many social media sites offer a lead generation platform where the user does not have to leave the platform in order to input their contact information. This differs from having a user click a link to your website or landing page in order to collect their personal information. Lead generation is a great way to make your social media real by finding users who are so interested in your products or services that they are willing to give their phone number or email address.

The point in using analytics is that you have to figure out how you are going to evaluate your digital marketing campaigns in order to make sense for your specific business. While reach, engagement, and growth should apply as sound metrics for almost any digital marketing campaign, the idea is to ensure that you are getting a good return on your investment of resources. If all you care about is reach, then maybe that's all you want to evaluate. Most of the time, though, you are going to want to assess your campaigns using various metrics (at least a couple) so that you can learn and adjust. The longer you do it, the more data you have, and the better your digital marketing should be. Without assessment, you'll run digital marketing campaigns for extended periods of time and most likely end up with marginal results. If this happens, consider what elements you may be missing. Most of the time, you'll find that your lack a strategic plan and adequate analysis are the major culprits standing in the way of your success.

11

Budgeting and Why Marketing is Not Like Buying a Lottery Ticket

In the opening chapter of this book, I stated that "marketing is not like buying a lottery ticket, but more like a 401k." I'd like to expand on this idea. What I mean is that marketing is not an extra thing you do when you have extra time or money to spend. Marketing is a thing you should *always* be doing and allocating resources toward, one way or another. Marketing doesn't always work the way you want it to, but what does? I've always found it odd how a business owner will go into a tirade over a marketing project that didn't work but act perfectly calm and collected when another aspect of his or her business fails just the same. I think that most business owners have such a short leash when it comes to marketing because they don't understand it, and people fear what they don't understand.

Marketing is an investment, not a lottery ticket, and it needs to be handled as such. An investment is something that pays off over the long haul but doesn't necessarily always provide positive returns at every checkpoint along the way. Most business owners treat marketing as a lottery ticket where they spend X dollars and expect Y in return. When this doesn't work, they fire X and move onto Z. If you find yourself doing this more often than not, I implore you to take a step back and analyze the situation and figure out what might be going on with U.

As I hope you have gathered from the book thus far, marketing is a *process*. I was drawn to marketing in the first place because I viewed marketing as the creation of a brand-new idea, over and over again. Compare this to a baker using different ingredients to create something delicious. Their craft requires skill and mastery, of course, but no one would fault a baker if a few of their culinary treats were less-than-ideal every once in a while. How else would the baker know if their creations were satisfactory without somebody tasting them in the first place?

This is where you want to be with your marketing; you want to be in a position where you have a skilled professional executing your marketing, all while using a strategic plan with adequate budgets and analysis. However, if you continually change the marketer (or the baker) without giving their efforts an appropriate amount of time to show results, then you will always assume that the marketer is the issue. A situation like this can be detrimental to your marketing because usually there is a learning curve associated with any marketing person working on a brand for the first time. Just as you need to educate yourself about marketing and learn which process the marketer is using, the marketing person also needs to learn about your business and your brand in order to be useful. Switching marketing people too frequently is sort of like the general manager of a sports team changing the coach every two years because the team never wins. Although the general manager is the one ultimately responsible for providing the coach with the players and adequate resources to do the job well, if he or she continually fires the coach, then he or she is, perhaps incorrectly, assuming that the coach is to blame. In some cases, this may be true, but in other cases, the problem may be attributed to a lack of consistency and a plan that has not yet been fully developed.

HOW MUCH MONEY SHOULD I SPEND ON MY CAMPAIGNS?

I've already discussed at length how to budget for your specific audience, but how do you figure out how many actual marketing dollars to spend? You do this by deciding how much of your total revenue you want to invest in marketing for a period of time and then evaluate the results. For most businesses, this is going to be a percentage of total revenue for the year, such as 2% - 5%. This system seems to work best because it is based on actual revenue, for which the marketing department would be partially responsible. This means that if I budget X % for my business based on Y revenue, and I don't hit Y revenue, then I'll get a new version of X. You can project your marketing spending based on your revenue projections and build in checkpoints (months, quarters, etc.) along the way. Adjusting your marketing dollars according to your revenue at those checkpoints is a great way to ensure that you always have a consistent marketing presence. However you intend to do this, or however it makes sense for your business, be sure to commit to something realistic and ample and to stick to your commitment. I know that marketing is one of the first things to go when times are tough, but try to keep your efforts as consistent as possible.

HOW TO FAIL AT MARKETING

The classic **shotgun approach** to marketing (which is what a lot of businesses are doing) is a perfect example of what *not to do*. This "approach" involves throwing out bunch of marketing materials in a short amount of time and expecting big results. This hardly ever works and, even if it does, it is still short-sided. Think about it: what is the most valuable aspect of running successful short-term marketing campaigns? The answer, of course, is that you have created a successful marketing equation. Why you wouldn't want to scale and build on that success for long term growth is beyond me. Remember that you can spend $1 on a lottery ticket and win millions if you're lucky, but the odds are very much against you. The same is true for marketing: don't expect to spend $100 on a marketing campaign and magically expect to get $10,000 of business in return. It simply doesn't work that way. Most times, the shotgun approach is a giant waste of time and resources for everyone involved. It usually means an angry business owner or a stressed-out general manager reacting emotionally and taking out his or her frustrations on the marketing itself. These types of marketing blitzes are typically neither strategic nor well thought out. They fail to use the ample resources needed to make them useful in the first place, so it's no wonder they don't usually work.

For example, Ray's carpet cleaning business is having a terrible month in terms of revenue, and Ray wants to bump up his sales. He asks his secretary to work with his intern and put out an offer on their social media pages for 50% off of carpet cleaning next week. He also gives them a $100 budget to boost the posts. Ray's Carpet Cleaning has a minimal following on social media and hasn't posted anything for six months. Ray's secretary and intern go ahead and post. They boost the posts, but nobody responds, and they don't get any additional business. Ray gets angry and decides that social media marketing doesn't work. He decides that his secretary and intern are both terrible at marketing. This is a lottery ticket approach to marketing: a "hope and pray" mentality. Hopefully, after reading this book, you've come to know better. There are dozens of reasons why this campaign didn't work, but ultimately the culprit is that Ray has not done a good job of investing in his marketing over time, so when he has something to say, nobody cares. He doesn't even have a marketing professional to rely on when he needs one. So, in this case anyway, he's stuck with his secretary and his intern.

If Ray had planned out his marketing using the 5 Steps and had given the process some time and attention, he would have been in a much better place to drive revenue when he needed it. In my opinion, one of the most detrimental things Ray does in this short example is to assume that his customers are avoiding purchasing his service this month because of the price. He proves this by offering a 50% off discount and nothing else. While a sale price *can* be an excellent incentive that drives revenue at times, it is not the only way. If, however, Ray was following a strategic plan over time, eventually he would *know* what his customers want in terms of a promotion. Price is not necessarily the number one culprit.

Another example is Sarah's Boutique, who is having a big one-day sale as part of a broader, city-wide promotion. Sarah is having a hard time deciding what to offer, so she procrastinates in putting any communication out to her customers. While many of the stores downtown are pushing the weekend sale, Sarah does not participate in any of the city-wide corporate advertising. While having a conversation with one of her neighboring businesses who has been promoting the event, Sarah decides to offer a free accessory item with any purchase over $50 during the city-wide promotion. Sarah has a decent following on social media and posts regularly. She contacts her graphic designer and asks for a flyer, social media graphics, and a beautiful graphic for her website. Sarah goes back and forth with her designer over the look of the graphics. Though she finally agrees on something that she likes, she receives all of the materials the day before the event. Sarah then goes ahead and posts. She knows that boosts work well, so she throws in a few hundred dollars. The day of the sale, Sarah gets a few customers in her shop who ask about the free accessory advertised on the flyer in the window, but only one customer comes in because of the social media post and none from the website. Therefore, Sarah actually *loses* money on her promotion.

Even though Sarah had a consistent social media presence, she did not have a system set up to enact advertising when she needed it. While she was able to get *something* out to her customers, she did not have enough time to penetrate them with advertising. The majority of the social media content Sarah puts out is all pictures taken with her cell phone. She rarely asks for graphics or updates her website. Because of this, Sarah's graphic team was very slow in producing graphics for her. They had to sort through several rounds of drafts before settling upon a design that Sarah liked. Sarah felt confident that once she received an excellent graphic to post on social media and on her website, this would be enough to make an impact, but it wasn't. She thought that a few hundred dollars for one day would do the trick, but it didn't. She also assumed that because her customers would see the promotion on her website that it would work well, but it didn't. Posting something on your website only has value when you have the right people looking. Otherwise, it's just a waste of time.

What Sarah needed to do was to use variable content over two weeks or so, in order to promote the sale to her customers. She also needed to take advantage of the city's co-op advertising and to be sure that her offer was adequately represented among everybody else's. She needed to have a good working relationship with her graphic arts team in order to produce ample content in a timely manner. She also needed to know the analytics of her website and understand how many people were actually visiting her site on a daily or weekly basis. Sarah reacted emotionally after speaking with her neighboring business owner who had been investing marketing dollars in the city-wide sale for weeks. She used a shotgun approach to a layup marketing opportunity, and, because of this, she saw abysmal results. When budgeting for marketing, always consider the time you'll need to penetrate your defined audience with your message. Getting this right takes some trial and error, but it is typically very scalable once you've figure it out. From the previous examples, if Ray had run various promotions in the past, he might have found that the message of "Buy One Room, Get One Room Free" worked better with his audience, even though a "50% off" message is saying essentially the same thing. A message that results in a strong call-to-action is what counts. Moreover, if Sarah had been consistently using varied content and she and her graphic designer had figured out a graphic style that her audience responded to well, they could have significantly improved the situation. Firstly, the designer would have known precisely what to create for Sarah's audience in order to promote the sale and, as a result, Sarah would have received the content much sooner. Secondly, Sarah and her designer would have known what kind of graphics would work most effectively, even within a short time frame. Lastly, if Sarah and her designer had paid attention to her website statistics, they would have known that her web traffic had been slow, and they would have spent very little time working on a website graphic. They may have skipped a graphic altogether and simply made sure that it was listed on her calendar somewhere. If they had followed these steps, Sarah's designer wouldn't have wasted their time on things that don't matter, and Sarah wouldn't have spent money paying for something that made little to no impact.

I hope you can see, now, that a strategic approach to marketing is always a much more valuable use of your hard-earned resources and that marketing, in most cases, should not be treated like a lottery ticket. Treat marketing like an investment in your business. Just like any financial investment, you want to have a strategy and track the analytics along the way. You'll have some good weeks and some bad ones, but if you learn and grow from your mistakes, you'll come out on top at the end of the year.

12

Two Very Important Words: Intentionality and Consistency

When it comes to digital marketing (or any marketing for that matter), the importance of consistency and intentionality cannot be overstated. In all my years of marketing, these have been the two most common reasons for success and the most common reasons for failure. Let's explore each one a little further.

Intentionality is an incredibly powerful digital marketing tool and one that many businesses do not employ. Intentionality is the act of posting content that is relevant to your business and avoiding filler content as much as possible. **Filler content** refers to generic social media posts that have no reason for existing aside from just being there. This kind of posting is usually done by managers who want to check "posting" off their to-do list and run their social media pages on a low-effort "maintenance program." This approach typically goes hand-in-hand with social media scheduling software that lets you schedule posts days or weeks in advance. This automation can be done by either a person or some kind of artificial intelligence. While this type of posting does lead to a feeling that your pages have been attended to, it fails to make any kind of impact on your audience. This makes the exercise pretty much pointless. Too many times, business owners opt for the easy, cookie-cutter approach to digital marketing and then expect a big return. Think about the most critical aspects of your life; how many of these would you automate? Your finances, your relationships, your taxes? Or are these things so important that they require time, energy, and sometimes even spending money on resources or experts? Marketing should be no different.

Scheduling software is helpful and can be an excellent tool to help streamline your digital marketing, but it cannot become a substitute for proper marketing execution. Scheduling too far out and too often will also not allow you to react to what might be going on with your business in real-time. While there is nothing wrong with scheduling out some of your high-level content, often your "real-time" content will be most impactful. More importantly, any marketing manager working on your social media pages *needs* to have their eye on your social media pages and daily, if possible. They need to see what the posts look like to the users in the audience. They need to understand which posts are gaining engagement. They need to interact with the audience in order to drive further engagement and growth. All of this is really hard to accomplish in one hour a week using scheduling software. Take the time to see what your pages look like to a new user and, as a result, see how your business might be perceived as a brand. The only way to do this is to actually take the time to go to your pages, look them over, and spend some time evaluating each aspect.

Back in my days of restaurant management, I was in charge of running a bakery/cafe concept near Chicago. Every morning we had to lay out fresh products in our bakery case, arranging them just so, so that the customers would see what we wanted them to see. We, of course, arranged the products from behind the case in a way that we thought would look appealing to the customer on the other side. The only way to know how the bakery case would actually look to the customer, however, was to view the display from the customer's perspective. We had to stop what we were doing and walk to the other side of the case. This was the only way to know how we needed to adjust our products in order to ensure that they were appropriately displayed: move a bear claw a little to the left, bring the cinnamon rolls up to the front as the day wore on, etc. This is what you need to do with your social media and digital marketing: you need to go through the process, just as a customer would, to ensure that you are perceived in the way that you want.

Taking this example a step further, I would argue that another (and more fun) way to interpret the bakery case is for the bakery manager to taste the pastries for quality. For you, this means going through the process as a customer: from seeing the page, to clicking the ad, to filling out the landing page, etc. Far too often, business owners rely on third party companies to do this for them with very little oversight. Don't get me wrong, there are a ton of really great marketing companies out there, but you never know until you verify it for yourself.

I ran into one such situation where a business owner had spent close to $10,000 on digital ads and had received $0 in business in return. An outsourced company was running his marketing, and this particular business owner was not only clueless as to what he was paying for, but was too scared (or intimidated) to check out the situation for himself. Upon inspection, I discovered that his social media pages looked great, and his ads were a thing of beauty. The budget he was spending seemed to be more than sufficient, and the target audience appeared to be right on the money. The click-through rates on his ads were above-average, and his CPM seemed right in line with what other businesses in his industry were spending. The problem was related to the landing page created by the company executing his marketing campaign. The page in of itself was fine, but his website was not mobile-friendly, meaning that it was almost impossible to read on a mobile device. Checking his stats, 85% of the users who clicked on his ads were doing so on a mobile device. So, I showed the business owner what his pages and advertisements looked like on a phone. The user was brought to a barely legible page that was almost impossible to navigate. This is an example of a sound marketing campaign that *almost* worked, but nobody ever took the time to actually go through the process as a customer would. That made all the difference in the world.

I want to be clear; if you are posting on social media just to post *something*, you are most likely posting to the wind and probably wasting your time. Typically, only a targeted marketing program with intentional posts will produce results worth your time and energy. Remember that digital marketing is, in most instances, your most efficient and effective form of marketing, but only if it is executed properly using the appropriate time and resources. Be sure to treat it as you would any other form of marketing. This will require your full attention at times. Don't fall into the trap of thinking that there is a new and amazing "automated" way to get amazing results. Use your head the same way you would for any other business or financial decision and realize that marketing is, essentially, no different.

Consistency goes hand-in-hand with intentionality. When used together, these two form the cornerstone of successful marketing. You want to *regularly* post intentional content about your business to your audience using a strategic plan. This is how you achieve success in the world of social media. You need to treat your business as a year-round brand, regardless of what kind of business you have. Many companies run their marketing on a "binge and purge cycle" or use a "start and stop approach." These approaches involve spending lots of energy and resources on digital marketing for a short amount time, followed by a period of doing nothing before resuming with another push, and so on. When doing this, you're half-way right in the sense that you do need to allocate resources differently at different times of the year. What you shouldn't do, though, is turn your marketing off entirely before turning it back on. Work hard and get creative to figure out ways of making your business a year-round brand. Doing so will help to keep your business or brand consistently at the top of customers' minds. This approach also helps to keep your audience engaged, which will help drive positive results towards your organic reach within the algorithm.

For some businesses, this can be a very trying exercise, and the idea of sitting in front of a blank computer or phone screen with nothing to post can be a little scary. Let's look into a business we'll call The Fryburg Turtles Baseball Team: a made-up minor league team that operates only four months of the year at their local stadium. How can they become a year-round brand? Let's have a look.

January

"Best Year Ever Campaign" for New Year's Eve - Fans post about their favorite experiences from the previous year and win prizes.

"Winter Ball Highlights" - Keep up with what the players do during the wintertime; show up at a school and bring hot chocolate to the teachers to thank them for supporting your reading program.

February

"For The Love Of the Game Promotion" for Valentine's Day – Give away pairs of tickets to the upcoming season when couples engage with your posts; get to know the team's announcers; highlight your reading program with a cross-promotion at local libraries.

March

Highlight charities you're working with in the coming year; create trivia questions about the team with prizes; get to know the general manager; get to know the managers; push season ticket sales.

April & May

Introduce this year's roster; push season ticket and individual game sales; introduce new vendors at the stadium; introduce new activities at the stadium; highlight special days at the ballpark for this coming year; push corporate and suite sales.

June - BASEBALL GAMES ETC.

July - BASEBALL GAMES ETC.

August - BASEBALL GAMES ETC.

September - BASEBALL GAMES ETC.

October

Post end of year stats including how many hot dogs you sold, home runs you hit, miles you traveled, etc.

"Guess Who Campaign" for Halloween - Have players, managers and front office dress up in costumes and have fans guess who they are to win prizes; record thank you messages from players, managers and front office to the fans thanking them for a great year.

November

"ThanksForGiving Month Campaign" for Thanksgiving - Highlight how much money you gave away this season to local charities, highlighting each local charity you work with and a few essential people at each; Black Friday sale on merchandise and tickets.

December

Christmas and Cyber Monday Sale on merchandise and tickets; send a Santa Claus out with your Mascot to make a few appearances in the community for videos and pictures; get the front office staff together and sing a few Christmas carols.

Hopefully, you can see how a little bit of creativity can result is some fantastic social media content for your digital marketing channels. While this might be an extreme example, any business can benefit from creating content year-round. If you're still having trouble with this, go back to the three brand standards that you defined in Step #3, then brainstorm a few ways that you could communicate each one creatively. Figure out which of those ideas you can execute properly, then use each one to fill gaps in your year-long calendar where you may have nothing to say. If you do this exercise the right way, you'll probably come up with some of the best social media content ideas you've ever had. I can't stress this enough, use digital marketing as an opportunity to get creative about your business. It is an excellent outlet for executing almost anything you can think of, so don't miss out!

YOUR DIGITAL FOOTPRINT

To tie all of this together, consider the idea of *mise en place*, meaning "everything in its place." This idea is crucial to your digital branding because, odds are, you are going to be marketing on several different platforms and outlets all at the same time, which will make up what I am going to refer to as your **digital footprint**. Your digital footprint is made up of all of your digital marketing efforts, and here is where you need to be sure that you have everything in its place. I can't tell you the number of times I have consulted on a digital marketing project only to find that the company has three different logos appearing in various locations of their digital platforms. This is not only confusing to your customer or user; it makes you look unprofessional. When attempting to maintain consistency among all of aspects of your digital footprint, be sure to consider the following sources, all of which make up your digital marketing presence.

1. Website

2. Social Media Pages

3. App

4. Review Sites

5. Search Engine Listings

Just as you want to take a step back and ensure that your marketing equations work, you also want to be sure that your branding is consistent across all of your digital marketing channels. Strive to make sure that your logos, graphics, links, hours, are accurate, and that they information look the same across all of these channels. I remember one instance where I received a call from a client who was very upset that we had posted the wrong date for his business event on one of his social media pages. I was quick to apologize, but after reviewing the matter further, I noticed that the business had posted two different dates and times on their website. One was done by the business owner and the other by his web company. We pulled data from the main link on the homepage, which had been incorrect. This mistake could have been a major catastrophe had customers come in on the wrong day for the event. So, I implore you to have checks and balances in place to ensure that all of the information you are providing in the digital space is consistent.

You also want to keep an eye on **dead links:** web links that either go to the wrong place or don't go anywhere at all. Far too many times, I find businesses with links on their website that are old and broken or with social media icons on their homepages that go to the wrong social media page or no page at all. As previously stated, if you are going to attempt to market your business on a digital platform, be intentional about doing so. Just posting a link on your website to a social media page does not accomplish anything unless you intend to use that social media page as a marketing outlet. If not, remove it. If, for some reason, you decide not to use any social media pages at all, then please go ahead and remove the links altogether. Trust me, you're better off.

This concept also applies to making sure that you are keeping your digital marketing platforms up to date with current information. If you had a big event and it's now over, please remove it from your website. Nothing says, "I have a terrible problem with attention to details," like old information sitting on a website. If you have a promotion and have pinned a graphic to the top of your social media pages for maximum value, please don't leave it there for months at a time. Create a new graphic once in a while so that your social media pages look professional. Otherwise, you are most likely going to give off a negative impression. It communicates to your users that you don't care enough to fix these errors, don't follow through, and don't have the resources needed in order to take care of something that you committed to accomplishing. Who wants that?

Following through goes hand in hand with intentionality and consistency. One of the mortal sins of digital marketing is having social media pages that have not been used in a long time. I never understood why any business would want to link a current or potential customer to a social media page that hasn't posted anything for weeks, months, or even years. Many times, the businesses themselves don't even know they are doing this. They already have their links pre-set in every email blast, newsletter, and web page that they create. Do you realize that you are telling the user that *you don't care?* Does posting an active link to a random, forgotten web page somewhere get a person to somehow care about it? This situation is far too common, and the only effect this can possibly even achieve is negative branding for your business. Quite frankly, it makes you look stupid. Again, you don't have to market on every social media platform, but when you do decide to commit to one or two, do your best to see it through and always be professional.

I want to get back to the idea of mise en place as it relates to your posts and ads. One of the most beneficial aspects of digital marketing is the ability to start and stop a campaign whenever you want. This shift is a significant departure from traditional advertising where, most of the time, you had one shot at delivering creative content. Sure, you could always stop and start a radio or TV campaign by pulling the commercial, re-producing it, and then starting it again, but in some cases that could take weeks and also cost you a lot of money.

The availability of real-time analytics is another feature that traditional advertising never had, and you should take full advantage of this. When you go through the 5 Steps to create your marketing campaigns in any capacity, you don't have to let them run for weeks or months at a time before making adjustments. Run your paid ads for a couple of days at an accelerated rate, or post a few different pieces of content on your pages for a few days, and see if you get any organic response. Then, interpret the data as it applies to the goal of your campaign, make some adjustments, and keep going.

Remember that every word, picture, emoji, link, page layout, video etc. can and *will* make a difference in terms of getting users to do what you want them to do. In my experience, I have found that sometimes the slightest adjustment can have the most significant impact. I recall one project where we were having a tough time getting users to sign up for tours at a particular private school, which was the goal of our campaign. We decided to run the campaign for a week and made some adjustments to the audience. We ran the campaign for another few days and then made a few adjustments to the content. We ran this for *another* few days and made some adjustments to the landing page. Suddenly, we had a marketing equation that worked for our target audience. In this case (as with many cases), the adjustments that we made were minimal: rewriting the wording, adjusting the positioning of text overlay on the graphic, and moving the position of the video on the landing page. These adjustments may seem small, and they are, but they made a significant impact on our target audience and eventually inspired them to do exactly what we wanted them to do.

When you are intentional and consistent with your digital marketing, it is much easier to achieve positive engagement and branding from your posts. This ensures a consistent digital footprint. Don't fool yourself; your audience will be able to tell the difference between intentional and unintentional content. Besides, most digital marketing outlets will benefit significantly from a brand that respects their audience enough to spend the right amount of time and resources communicating to them properly, as opposed to just using old, generic, passive, or non-impactful content. I implore you to take some pride in your marketing: your audience will notice, and your business will benefit.

13

The Most Important Word: Execution

Whenever I have the opportunity to speak to a group of marketing students, I always ask them the same question: "What is the number one, most important aspect of marketing?" The two most common answers I usually receive are creativity and branding, with relationships coming in at a close third. While all of these are essential parts of the marketing equation, I would argue none of these is the most critical aspect. The answer I am always looking for is *execution*. I would say that execution is not only the most important aspect of marketing, but it is also probably numbers two through ten as well. I want to explain this idea with a story which may or may not be a real-life example…

Joe is the marketing manager for a chain of restaurants in Chicago. One day during a visit to one of his company's restaurants, an employee makes a suggestion that sounds like an excellent marketing idea. At the next executive meeting, Joe pitches the idea to the corporate team, and everyone loves it. It is so great, in fact, that the owners pick up the idea and begin to expand on it. The entire team, from operations to accounting, is now discussing this new idea and everyone is putting in their two cents. At the end of the meeting, the team agrees that this new idea is going to be the company's main marketing push during the next quarter. The idea itself involves a new menu item: a combination of two current menu items which results in an entirely new product. With the dates and budgets set, Joe is now tasked with rolling out this new marketing campaign.

As we've already discussed at length, Joe is going to use the 5 Steps to execute his marketing campaign. Let's assume that he has already gone through each step and has a strategy ready to go. Now, let's look at what Joe has to do in order to execute the plan.

a. Work with the accounting team to ensure the new menu item will be profitable

b. Work with the culinary team to ensure the new menu item will work operationally

c. Ensure the new menu item is added to the restaurants' POS (Point of Sale) systems

d. Update the printable menus for the next quarter with the new menu item

e. Update the online menus for the next quarter with the new menu item

f. Make sure all of the restaurants' delivery partners' online menus are updated with the new menu item for next quarter

g. Arrange to have professional pictures taken of the new menu item

h. Arrange to have a professional video taken of the new menu item

i. Arrange to have creative collateral (graphics etc.) designed for the website

j.   Arrange to have creative collateral (graphics etc.) designed for each of the restaurants' social media platforms

k.   Arrange to have creative collateral (graphics etc.) designed for the restaurants' menu boards

l.   Arrange to have creative collateral (graphics etc.) designed to promote the new menu item within the four walls of the restaurant

m.   Plan a media buy (radio, television, etc.) for the upcoming quarter with collateral about the new menu item

n.   Plan a digital marketing buy (Facebook, YouTube, etc.) for the upcoming quarter with collateral about the new menu item

o.   Plan email blasts to the restaurants' current customers announcing the new menu item

A plan like this is what marketing is all about. It's about executing the communication of a creative message with the intent of branding a business and driving revenue. While creativity, branding, and relationships are critical building blocks that will ultimately lead to the success of this campaign, neither is individually more important than the execution of the campaign as a whole. If, for example, Joe forgot to do (g) (have professional pictures taken), then he would not be able to show his customers pictures of the new menu item, nor would he be able to represent the company's brand standard of food within other aspects of the marketing campaign. If Joe forgot to do (c) (ensure the new menu item is available on the restaurants' POS) on launch day, none of the customers would be able to order and pay for the menu item in the first place. The point is that every step in the execution of your marketing is essential, but no single step is more important than another. It is the skillful execution of the entire process where the real marketing magic happens.

This type of execution plan is essentially a marketing plan. Some of the steps in a marketing plan are marketing action steps while some are not. **Marketing action steps** are marketing campaigns within a marketing plan. The other stages of the marketing campaign are **action steps** but are not necessarily marketing in nature. In our example above, steps (a), (b), and (c) are action steps, while steps (d) through (o) are marketing action steps. You apply the 5 Step process we learned about earlier in the book to each of the marketing action steps within the plan.

For example, apply what you've learned in this book to compare step (n) (planning a digital marketing buy) with step (o) (plan an email blast campaign) using the 5 Steps. During step #1 (Find the Right Audience), you will have a direct contrast. The digital media buy you are planning in step (n) is going out to a mass of people, many of whom are *not* your current customers. Compare this to step (o) where you are creating a marketing campaign to send information about your restaurant to people who have opted in and are, presumably, your current customers. Besides the difference between purchasing Facebook and Google Ads versus email blasts, when you get to step #2 (Create the Right Content), the content of your messaging will be completely different. One audience is familiar with your business and one is not. Your messaging to each must be done with the appropriate amount of detail and branding. The elements in step #3 (Promote Your Business as a Brand) should be the same for both, as your restaurant has a set of brand standards that do not change.

The resource allocation in step #4 (Use Ample Resources) will be completely different. You will want to spend lots of time figuring out how much money to budget for your digital media buy. Your email blasts will most likely already be set up on an email server, with the monthly cost already built-in. The analytics in step #5 (Analyze Your Results) will also be very different for each of these campaigns as well. In measuring your digital ad campaigns in step (n), you are going to be measuring the reach, engagement, growth, and frequency, as well as the CPC, PPC, etc. While measuring the success of your email marketing campaign in step (o), you will most likely be measuring the percentage of emails opened as well as the number of click-throughs and shares, etc.

I hope that you can see the power of applying the 5 Steps to your marketing campaigns, and the ways in which you can use these steps to build an entire marketing plan. By doing so, you can market to different audiences using various forms of content, varying levels of resources allocation, and different analytical metrics. Don't get me wrong, this example is, of course, a company that has lots of resources and a reasonably strong reach within the market, but the same lessons can be applied to any size business, large or small. You may have an upstart company that only has one or two marketing action steps to accomplish, but the equations do not change.

While most people (including the students I mentioned earlier) say that creativity is the essential aspect of marketing, I want you to notice where the creative elements emerged in this example. The original idea itself came from a non-marketing-department person and, in fact, from an hourly restaurant employee. Understand that there is no monopoly on creativity, and good marketing ideas can come from anywhere. Be sure to keep your eyes, ears, and mind open to what other people in your company, or even your customers, have to say. What they come up with might surprise you. The goal of the marketing professional is to take those creative ideas and turn them into real marketing campaigns that benefit the business.

In your digital marketing efforts, you are most likely going to be faced with situations where you think of or are given an excellent idea for your social media channels. Then, upon further review, you decide that, while the concept is great, it does not fit in with your digital marketing plan for one reason or another. It may be outside your brand standards, you may not have the budget needed to produce it, or you may not have the resources needed to execute it properly, etc. In these cases, let it go. Executing a successful digital marketing campaign is about running marketing effectively, and you can't always fit a square peg in a round hole. Some things sound great and will get you excited, but the real marketer in you will know better and usually, that's the right choice.

THE CREATIVITY CURSE

Another unusual element about creativity is that often people who say they are not creative are the most creative people of all. Many times the business owner will get frustrated and say something like, *"But that was my idea! Why am I paying everyone else to be creative!?"* The reason that business owners usually come up with the best ideas is, first of all, because they had to be skilled and successful enough at business to become the business owner in the first place. Secondly, they are, in many cases, putting lots of personal attributes into the business's brand (things they care about and value, etc.) and this, in a weird way, makes *them* as a person the brand. They are also probably the most worried about finances as they usually have the most to either lose or gain from the failure or success of the business. Because of this, they are the ones thinking about the company more than anyone else. Therefore, they will usually be the ones to come up with the most creative ideas for their business as a result of this ongoing thought.

You could argue that creativity and budgets are the reason that some marketing campaigns are more successful than others. In some cases, you might be right. Don't discount, however, other aspects of those campaigns that played into it their success in the first place. It's sort of like watching a great movie and giving all of the credit to the actors when, in fact, hundreds, if not thousands, of other people were involved in supporting the actors and, therefore, helping to make the movie successful. It's also like why the same five or ten people out of thousands end up at the final table of the World Series of Poker every year, when some people claim poker is just a game of dumb luck. It's not a matter of luck; it's a matter of skill and strategy well played. The same is true for your marketing campaigns. It is always the execution of your marketing that will bring you success, and that should never be understated.

14

Words of Encouragement: This is Not Rocket Science

First of all, congratulations on finishing this book! I really appreciate you taking the time to read it. I hope that this has helped to provide you with a strategic approach to digital marketing. For some of you, these ideas may come easily while for others, this may feel like trying to learn a new language. Either way, please remember that while marketing can be complicated at times, it is far from rocket science. If there's one thing I've experienced over the years that always pays off, it's that when people use their instincts to make sound marketing decisions good things happen. Therefore, I implore you (especially those of you who are struggling) to take a deep breath and go with what you know. You probably know more about your business than anyone, and you probably already have a lot of ideas for your digital marketing campaigns. I want to be the first to encourage you to act on those instincts. If nothing else, use what you've learned in this book to vet your ideas and see how or if they fit into a proven marketing strategy. Most likely, some will work in one form or another by just adapting them into a proper marketing equation by using the 5 Step process.

Remember that marketing is no different from any other aspect of your business, and you may want to outsource it at times. Don't feel bad about it; we all have to outsource aspects of our business from time to time. I know enough about accounting to be dangerous, but I pay a professional accountant to do my bookkeeping, taxes, etc. in order to ensure that it's done right. I pay them for their expertise and for their experience. The same can be true for your marketing. If this is the case, however, don't do it blindly. Hold your marketing team to the standards you've read about here.

However you decide to go about executing your marketing in the future, remember to always strive to have *marketing* conversations with your team. This means going over the aspects laid out in the 5 Steps and understanding how each fits into your business. Too many times, business owners and marketing people want to spend too much time discussing things that don't matter. Hire technical people to do the technical work, hire marketing people to do the marketing work, and hold each of them accountable for what they produce and the results they achieve. Be sure to have a clear idea of the results you are looking for, and make sure everyone knows how to define success along the way.

Whether you're a natural marketer, or whether you're scared to post for the first time, you *can* do this. The discipline of marketing has been around for decades. It has helped to build businesses, drive revenue, and achieve brand awareness for just about any product, service, or organization you can imagine. It can and will work for you too. Get out there and apply what you've learned from this book to your digital marketing campaigns and take the time to do it the right way. I have used this process to help hundreds of businesses achieve success in the world of digital marketing, and I am confident that it will work for you too. Good luck!

Important Marketing Words (for reference)

A ll of the marketing and business terms found in this book will all be defined by me. I realize that for some of you, this may be the first time you are being introduced to certain topics. Therefore, I wanted to provide you with a list of terms you could refer to while reading this book. I hope this helps!

ADS

social media content geared towards a specific audience that you spend money on.

AFFILIATIONS

groups of people, publications, or associations that your target audience belongs to or follows.

B-ROLL

generic footage used on the screen, usually as a backdrop while someone is talking.

BEHAVIORS

engagement traits of users on social media platforms

BLIPS

periods of time where your marketing performs well outside what you typically expect from your campaign, but the event is short-lived and quickly bounces back to normal.

BOOSTING

spending money on organic posts in order to show them to a target audience

BRANDING

elements that make up how your business or product is perceived.

BUDGET

the amount of money we are able to spend on our social media campaigns.

CADENCE

the rhythmic flow of your digital marketing

CALL TO ACTION

something that you ask a consumer to do such as come to an event, purchase a new menu item, use a coupon, sign up for a rewards program, or follow you on Facebook.

COLD BRANDS (OR BUSINESSES)

where most consumers, or target audience, have very little to no prior knowledge of the brand or business

COMPETITIVE ADVANTAGE

how your business competes in your industry or what you can offer the customer that your competition (replacement businesses) cannot.

COMMUNITY MANAGEMENT

an approach to digital marketing whereby you spend time building relationships with individual users and groups.

CONSISTENCY (MARKETING APPROACH)

regularly posting to your social media pages.

CONTESTS

asking your audience to respond to a topic with some kind of an incentive to do so

CONTROLLED VIDEO

where you have complete control over the environment.

CONVERSIONS

a user-defined call-to-action.

COST PER CLICK (CPC)

the amount of money you pay for a user to click on your content.

CROSS-PLATFORM AFFILIATIONS

a way to use contacts from another source by uploading them to a new source.

CUSTOMER RELATIONSHIP MARKETING

the function by which businesses provide an op-in service for their customers to receive information about the company.

DARK ADS

ads that reach the target audience, but do not show up on the timeline of a business.

DEAD LINKS

web links that either go to the wrong place or don't go anywhere at all.

DIGITAL FOOTPRINT

a make-up of all of your digital marketing efforts

ENGAGEMENT

the action of someone taking an interest in your social media posts, or interacting with your content.

EMOJIS

pictures in the format of text that convey a feeling, meaning, or idea.

FILLER CONTENT

generic social media posts that have no reason for existing aside from just being there.

GEO-FENCING

sending users a message through a digital platform, but only if they enter a specific geographic location.

GEO-FILTERING

a filter (or picture frame of sorts) that users can only get when they are in or around your specific business.

GEO-TARGETING

segmenting your audience based on where they live, work, etc.

GROCERY PRODUCT (MARKETING CATEGORY CLASSIFICATION)

frequent purchases that require small amounts of resources, and do not typically require much time or energy to procure.

GROWTH

is the metric used to track how many new followers (or fans) you earn as a result of engagement with your social media marketing campaigns.

HASHTAGS

a # in front of a word or phrase that are searchable

INTERESTS

things users follow or like on a social media platform

IMPRESSIONS

content appearing to a user.

INTENTIONAL MARKETING (APPROACH)

the act of posting content that is relevant to your business and avoiding filler content as much as possible.

JEWELRY PRODUCT (MARKETING CATEGORY CLASSIFICATION)

as an infrequent purchase that most people do not think about often, is only relevant in certain situations, and typically requires more effort and resources from the consumer than other products and services.

LANDING PAGE

is a single-page website that has one specific purpose.

LEADS

specific information given by a user, requesting a follow-up; internal or external

LIVE VIDEO

broadcasting in real time.

LOCATION-BASED TAGGING (OR CHECK-IN)

where users use their location-based mobile device to virtually check-in at a business or virtually tag that business in a social media post.

MAGIC FUNCTION APPROACH

the false assumption that a business or product that has not been previously positioned on a particular marketing platform should produce positive results simply by virtue of appearing via the said medium for the first time.

MARKETING ACTION STEPS

marketing campaigns within a marketing plan.

NON-PRODUCED VIDEO

lower quality than professional video, usually done with a phone or tablet

ORGANIC REACH

the number of people who see your content without you having to pay for it directly.

PAY PER CLICK

ads you only pay when someone clicks on your ad.

PLATFORM (OR MARKETING PLATFORM)

a digital marketing application or site (e.g. Facebook, Google, Instagram)

POSITIONING

distinct aspects of a brand that have become well-known in a particular audience's competitive set or mind.

POSTS

social media content that you *don't* spend money on and that achieve their value organically.

PRODUCED VIDEO

where you have a videographer or a professional camera, lights, sound, and a fully edited and finished product.

QUESTIONS (DIRECT OR IN-DIRECT)
asking your audience to respond to a topic, non-paid

RE-MARKETING

content marketed to users who have visited a specific website, or social media page

REACH

the amount of people you reach with your campaigns

REPLACEMENT BUSINESS

a similar business with similar offerings that could act as a replacement for another business in the consumer's mind.

RETURN ON INVESTMENT

a comparison between the amount of money you spend on something versus the amount of money you earned from it.

REVENUE

money you earn from doing business.

SEARCHING FOR THEM (MARKETING CATEGORY CLASSIFICATION)

the act of marketers searching for a specific audience on a marketing platform

SEARCHING FOR YOU (MARKETING CATEGORY CLASSIFICATION)

the act of users searching for a specific product, service or business on a marketing platform

SECONDARY AUDIENCE

an additional specific group of people you intend to reach with your marketing collateral, besides your target audience

SCOPE

the size of the marketing campaign in relation to the size of the product, service, or event.

SET BUDGET

a specific amount of money that you have to spend.

SHORTENED LINKS

reducing the size of long URL links

SHOTGUN MARKETING (APPROACH)

inconsistent marketing approach that involves throwing out bunch of marketing materials in a short amount of time and expecting big results.

SPAM

overly advertised content that nobody wants.

STATISTICS

numbers that you use to analyze the validity of your social media campaigns.

SUPPORTIVE MARKETING CAMPAIGN

a non-revenue driving campaign used to support a revenue driving campaign.

TARGET AUDIENCE

the specific group of people you intend to reach with your marketing collateral.

TEASE CAMPAIGN

pieces of marketing used to build interest in a business or product.

TRANSPARENT IMAGES

where the image or logo doesn't have any background.

TRENDS

extended periods of time where less-than-ideal, or overachieving numbers begin to become the norm.

UNCONTROLLED VIDEO

shoots where your business is operating, or your event is happening.

USER

a person who uses a digital marketing platform.

VARIED CONTENT

using a myriad of different kinds of content for marketing purposes. (images, videos, articles, etc.)

WATERMARK

a transparent graphic embedded in stock pictures which can only be removed when it is purchased from the source.

80/20 RULE

only 20% of people are going to read anything on your social media pages.

20/20 RULE

reach at least 20% of your target audience consistently, and then get 20% of those people to engage with your content regularly.

5 Step System Worksheet
(so you can follow along!)

CHAPTER 1

Business/Organization Name:

I am currently marketing on the following digital platforms:

Rate my knowledge 1 through 10 (1 I know nothing; 10 I am an expert)

A. Marketing in general -

B. Social Media Marketing -

C. Content Creation -

D. Marketing Strategy -

E. Marketing Budgeting -

I want to market my business/organization on the following digital marketing platforms:

CHAPTER 2

The 5 Step System is

1.

2.

3.

4.

5.

CHAPTER 3

Potential "Business Problems" of my marketing campaigns are:

Ideas for Posts (organic content):

Ideas for Ads (paid content):

Search for some groups on Facebook & LinkedIn (or other sites) and write down a few that makes sense for you to get involved with:

I enjoy networking in the physical world. Yes or No

I enjoy networking in the digital world. Yes or No

CHAPTER 4

My product or service is: **Jewelry or Groceries**

My brand is currently defined as the following terms/adjectives:

Call-To-Action Ideas for my campaigns:

My business is best suited for :

"I Am Searching For Them" or "They Are Searching For Me"

CHAPTER 5

The goal that most resonated with me was:

1. Build Revenue

2. Drive Awareness

3. Lead Generation

4. Keep Up With Your Competitors

5. A Progressive Marketing Action

6. Not Sure

I picked this one because?

CHAPTER 6

My Target Audience is (write a brief description):

Attributes of my Target Audience:

1. Demographic

2. Geographic

3. Interests

4. Job Titles

5. Behaviors

6. Affiliations

CHAPTER 7

The 80/20 Rule is?

Content Ideas for my product or service:

1. Images

2. Graphics

3. Landing Pages

4. Videos

5. Questions

6. Contests

7. Location Based Content

CHAPTER 8

Three things I want people to think about when they think about my business are:

1.

2.

3.

Currently, I think my marketing communicates the following attributes about my business:

How do your two answers above compare?

Where do you think you need to make changes?

CHAPTER 9

The total potential amount of people in my target audience is about:

The average CPM for my target audience is about:

The 20/20 Rule is:

CHAPTER 10

My goals is to Reach _____ (number) people on a monthly basis

Of those people, my goal is to get _____ percentage of them to engage with my content

My goal is to achieve _____ new followers (growth) on a monthly basis

Conversions for my business on digital platforms will be defined as:

I will verify the number of conversions by doing the following:

CHAPTER 11

I will budget my campaigns: (pick one)

Daily

Weekly

Monthly

Quarterly

Yearly

The budget for my advertising campaigns is:

_____ (dollars) per _____ (same as circled above)

CHAPTER 12

Content ideas for the next 12 months:

January   February

March   April

May   June

July   August

September   October

November   December

My digital footprint is made up of

1. (Website)

2. (Social Media Pages)

3. (App)

4. (Review Sites)

5. (Search Engine Listings)

CHAPTER 13

Marketing Action Steps I need to take to accomplish my goal:

Supportive Marketing Actions I need to take to accomplish my goal:

CHAPTER 14

Rate my knowledge 1 through 10 (1 I know nothing; 10 I am an expert)

A. Marketing in general -

B. Social Media Marketing -

C. Content Creation -

D. Marketing Strategy -

E. Marketing Budgeting -

Go back and look at how you scored yourself in Chapter 1 - did you improve?

Yes or No

What is the difference between posting and marketing?

After this reading this book I have learned: